ALZHEIMER'S DISEASE

THE ENCYCLOPEDIA OF
HEALTH

MEDICAL DISORDERS AND THEIR TREATMENT

Dale C. Garell, M.D. · General Editor

ALZHEIMER'S DISEASE

William A. Check

Introduction by C. Everett Koop, M.D., Sc.D.
Surgeon General, U.S. Public Health Service

CHELSEA HOUSE PUBLISHERS
New York Philadelphia

The goal of the ENCYCLOPEDIA OF HEALTH *is to provide general information in the ever-changing areas of physiology, psychology, and related medical issues. The titles in this series are not intended to take the place of the professional advice of a physician or other health-care professional.*

ON THE COVER: Photo by Bob Gomel

Chelsea House Publishers
EDITOR-IN-CHIEF: Nancy Toff
EXECUTIVE EDITOR: Remmel T. Nunn
MANAGING EDITOR: Karyn Gullen Browne
COPY CHIEF: Juliann Barbato
PICTURE EDITOR: Adrian G. Allen
ART DIRECTOR: Maria Epes
MANUFACTURING MANAGER: Gerald Levine

The Encyclopedia of Health
SENIOR EDITOR: Jane Larkin Crain

Staff for ALZHEIMER'S DISEASE
ASSOCIATE EDITOR: Paula Edelson
DEPUTY COPY CHIEF: Ellen Scordato
EDITORIAL ASSISTANTS: Susan DeRosa, Jennifer Trachtenberg
PICTURE RESEARCHER: Villette Harris
DESIGNER: Victoria Tomaselli
PRODUCTION COORDINATOR: Joseph Romano

3 5 7 9 8 6 4 2

Library of Congress Cataloging-in-Publication Data
Check, William A.
Alzheimer's disease.
(The Encyclopedia of health)
Bibliography: p.
Includes index.
Summary: Examines the effects, possible causes, diagnosis, and treatment of Alzheimer's disease and problems faced by families of the victims.
1. Alzheimer's disease—Juvenile literature.
[1. Alzheimer's disease] I. Title. II. Series.
RC523.C46 1988 618.97'683 88-16126
ISBN 0-7910-0056-7
0-7910-0483-X (pbk.)

CONTENTS

THE ENCYCLOPEDIA OF HEALTH

THE HEALTHY BODY

The Circulatory System
Dental Health
The Digestive System
The Endocrine System
Exercise
Genetics & Heredity
The Human Body: An Overview
Hygiene
The Immune System
Memory & Learning
The Musculoskeletal System
The Neurological System
Nutrition
The Reproductive System
The Respiratory System
The Senses
Speech & Hearing
Sports Medicine
Vision
Vitamins & Minerals

THE LIFE CYCLE

Adolescence
Adulthood
Aging
Childhood
Death & Dying
The Family
Friendship & Love
Pregnancy & Birth

MEDICAL ISSUES

Careers in Health Care
Environmental Health
Folk Medicine
Health Care Delivery
Holistic Medicine
Medical Ethics
Medical Fakes & Frauds
Medical Technology
Medicine & the Law
Occupational Health
Public Health

PSYCHOLOGICAL DISORDERS AND THEIR TREATMENT

Anxiety & Phobias
Child Abuse
Compulsive Behavior
Delinquency & Criminal Behavior
Depression
Diagnosing & Treating Mental Illness
Eating Habits & Disorders
Learning Disabilities
Mental Retardation
Personality Disorders
Schizophrenia
Stress Management
Suicide

MEDICAL DISORDERS AND THEIR TREATMENT

AIDS
Allergies
Alzheimer's Disease
Arthritis
Birth Defects
Cancer
The Common Cold
Diabetes
Drugs: Prescription & OTC
First Aid & Emergency Medicine
Gynecological Disorders
Headaches
The Hospital
Kidney Disorders
Medical Diagnosis
The Mind-Body Connection
Mononucleosis & Other Infectious Diseases
Nuclear Medicine
Organ Transplants
Pain
Physical Handicaps
Poisons & Toxins
Sexually Transmitted Diseases
Skin Diseases
Stroke & Heart Disease
Substance Abuse
Tropical Medicine

PREVENTION AND EDUCATION: THE KEYS TO GOOD HEALTH

C. Everett Koop, M.D., Sc.D.
Surgeon General,
U.S. Public Health Service

The issue of health education has received particular attention in recent years because of the presence of AIDS in the news. But our response to this particular tragedy points up a number of broader issues that doctors, public health officials, educators, and the public face. In particular, it points up the necessity for sound health education for citizens of all ages.

Over the past 25 years this country has been able to bring about dramatic declines in the death rates for heart disease, stroke, accidents, and, for people under the age of 45, cancer. Today, Americans generally eat better and take better care of themselves than ever before. Thus, with the help of modern science and technology, they have a better chance of surviving serious—even catastrophic—illnesses. That's the good news.

But, like every phonograph record, there's a flip side, and one with special significance for young adults. According to a report issued in 1979 by Dr. Julius Richmond, my predecessor as Surgeon General, Americans aged 15 to 24 had a higher death rate in 1979 than they did 20 years earlier. The causes: violent death and injury, alcohol and drug abuse, unwanted pregnancies, and sexually transmitted diseases. Adolescents are particularly vulnerable, because they are beginning to explore their own sexuality and perhaps to experiment with drugs. The need for educating young people is critical, and the price of neglect is high.

Yet even for the population as a whole, our health is still far from what it could be. Why? A 1974 Canadian government report attributed all death and disease to four broad elements: inadequacies in the health-care system, behavioral factors or unhealthy life-styles, environmental hazards, and human biological factors.

To be sure, there are diseases that are still beyond the control of even our advanced medical knowledge and techniques. And despite yearnings that are as old as the human race itself, there is no "fountain of youth" to ward off aging and death. Still, there is a solution to many of the problems that undermine sound health. In a word, that solution is prevention. Prevention, which includes health promotion and education, saves lives, improves the quality of life, and, in the long run, saves money.

In the United States, organized public health activities and preventive medicine have a long history. Important milestones include the improvement of sanitary procedures and the development of pasteurized milk in the late 19th century, and the introduction in the mid-20th century of effective vaccines against polio, measles, German measles, mumps, and other once-rampant diseases. Internationally, organized public health efforts began on a wide-scale basis with the International Sanitary Conference of 1851, to which 12 nations sent representatives. The World Health Organization, founded in 1948, continues these efforts under the aegis of the United Nations, with particular emphasis on combatting communicable diseases and the training of health-care workers.

But despite these accomplishments, much remains to be done in the field of prevention. For too long, we have had a medical care system that is science- and technology-based, focused, essentially, on illness and mortality. It is now patently obvious that both the social and the economic costs of such a system are becoming insupportable.

Implementing prevention—and its corollaries, health education and promotion—is the job of several groups of people:

First, the medical and scientific professions need to continue basic scientific research, and here we are making considerable progress. But increased concern with prevention will also have a decided impact on how primary-care doctors practice medicine. With a shift to health-based rather than morbidity-based medicine, the role of the "new physician" will include a healthy dose of patient education.

Second, practitioners of the social and behavioral sciences—psychologists, economists, city planners—along with lawyers, business leaders, and government officials—must solve the practical and ethical dilemmas confronting us: poverty, crime, civil rights, literacy, education, employment, housing, sanitation, environmental protection, health care delivery systems, and so forth. All of these issues affect public health.

Third is the public at large. We'll consider that very important group in a moment.

Fourth, and the linchpin in this effort, is the public health profession—doctors, epidemiologists, teachers—who must harness the professional expertise of the first two groups and the common sense and cooperation of the third, the public. They must define the problems statistically and qualitatively and then help us set priorities for finding the solutions.

To a very large extent, improving those statistics is the responsibility of every individual. So let's consider more specifically what the role of the individual should be and why health education is so important to that role. First, and most obviously, individuals can protect themselves from illness and injury and thus minimize their need for professional medical care. They can eat a nutritious diet, get adequate exercise, avoid tobacco, alcohol, and drugs, and take prudent steps to avoid accidents. The proverbial "apple a day keeps the doctor away" is not so far from the truth, after all.

Second, individuals should actively participate in their own medical care. They should schedule regular medical and dental checkups. Should they develop an illness or injury, they should know when to treat themselves and when to seek professional help. To gain the maximum benefit from any medical treatment that they do require, individuals must become partners in that treatment. For instance, they should understand the effects and side effects of medications. I counsel young physicians that there is no such thing as too much information when talking with patients. But the corollary is the patient must know enough about the nuts and bolts of the healing process to understand what the doctor is telling him. That is at least partially the patient's responsibility.

Education is equally necessary for us to understand the ethical and public policy issues in health care today. Sometimes individuals will encounter these issues in making decisions about their own treatment or that of family members. Other citizens may encounter them as jurors in medical malpractice cases. But we all become involved, indirectly, when we elect our public officials, from school board members to the president. Should surrogate parenting be legal? To what extent is drug testing desirable, legal, or necessary? Should there be public funding for family planning, hospitals, various types of medical research, and medical care for the indigent? How should we allocate scant technological resources, such as kidney dialysis and organ transplants? What is the proper role of government in protecting the rights of patients?

What are the broad goals of public health in the United States today? In 1980, the Public Health Service issued a report aptly entitled *Promoting Health-Preventing Disease: Objectives for the Nation.* This report expressed its goals in terms of mortality and in terms of intermediate goals in education and health improvement. It identified 15 major concerns: controlling high blood pressure; improving family planning; improving pregnancy care and infant health; increasing the rate of immunization; controlling sexually transmitted diseases; controlling the presence of toxic agents and radiation in the environment; improving occupational safety and health; preventing accidents; promoting water fluoridation and dental health; controlling infectious diseases; decreasing smoking; decreasing alcohol and drug abuse; improving nutrition; promoting physical fitness and exercise; and controlling stress and violent behavior.

For healthy adolescents and young adults (ages 15 to 24), the specific goal was a 20% reduction in deaths, with a special focus on motor vehicle injuries and alcohol and drug abuse. For adults (ages 25 to 64), the aim was 25% fewer deaths, with a concentration on heart attacks, strokes, and cancers.

Smoking is perhaps the best example of how individual behavior can have a direct impact on health. Today cigarette smoking is recognized as the most important single preventable cause of death in our society. It is responsible for more cancers and more cancer deaths than any other known agent; is a prime risk factor for heart and blood vessel disease, chronic bronchitis, and emphysema; and is a frequent cause of complications in pregnancies and of babies born prematurely, underweight, or with potentially fatal respiratory and cardiovascular problems.

Since the release of the Surgeon General's first report on smoking in 1964, the proportion of adult smokers has declined substantially, from 43% in 1965 to 30.5% in 1985. Since 1965, 37 million people have quit smoking. Although there is still much work to be done if we are to become a "smoke-free society," it is heartening to note that public health and public education efforts—such as warnings on cigarette packages and bans on broadcast advertising—have already had significant effects.

In 1835, Alexis de Tocqueville, a French visitor to America, wrote, "In America the passion for physical well-being is general." Today, as then, health and fitness are front-page items. But with the greater scientific and technological resources now available to us, we are in a far stronger position to make good health care available to everyone. And with the greater technological threats to us as we approach the 21st century, the need to do so is more urgent than ever before. Comprehensive information about basic biology, preventive medicine, medical and surgical treatments, and related ethical and public policy issues can help you arm yourself with the knowledge you need to be healthy throughout your life.

FOREWORD

Dale C. Garell, M.D.

Advances in our understanding of health and disease during the 20th century have been truly remarkable. Indeed, it could be argued that modern health care is one of the greatest accomplishments in all of human history. In the early 1900s, improvements in sanitation, water treatment, and sewage disposal reduced death rates and increased longevity. Previously untreatable illnesses can now be managed with antibiotics, immunizations, and modern surgical techniques. Discoveries in the fields of immunology, genetic diagnosis, and organ transplantation are revolutionizing the prevention and treatment of disease. Modern medicine is even making inroads against cancer and heart disease, two of the leading causes of death in the United States.

Although there is much to be proud of, medicine continues to face enormous challenges. Science has vanquished diseases such as smallpox and polio, but new killers, most notably AIDS, confront us. Moreover, we now victimize ourselves with what some have called "diseases of choice," or those brought on by drug and alcohol abuse, bad eating habits, and mismanagement of the stresses and strains of contemporary life. The very technology that is doing so much to prolong life has brought with it previously unimaginable ethical dilemmas related to issues of death and dying. The rising cost of health-care is a matter of central concern to us all. And violence in the form of automobile accidents, homicide, and suicide remain the major killers of young adults.

In the past, most people were content to leave health care and medical treatment in the hands of professionals. But since the 1960s, the consumer of medical care—that is, the patient—has assumed an increasingly central role in the management of his or her own health. There has also been a new emphasis placed on prevention: People are recognizing that their own actions can help prevent many of the conditions that have caused death and disease in the past. This accounts for the growing commitment to good nutrition and regular exercise, for the fact that more and more people are choosing not to smoke, and for a new moderation in people's drinking habits.

People want to know more about themselves and their own health. They are curious about their body: its anatomy, physiology, and biochemistry. They want to keep up with rapidly evolving medical technologies and procedures. They are willing to educate themselves about common disorders and diseases so that they can be full partners in their own health-care.

The ENCYCLOPEDIA OF HEALTH is designed to provide the basic knowledge that readers will need if they are to take significant responsibility for their own health. It is also meant to serve as a frame of reference for further study and exploration. The ENCYCLOPEDIA is divided into five subsections: The Healthy Body; The Life Cycle; Medical Disorders & Their Treatment; Psychological Disorders & Their Treatment; and Medical Issues. For each topic covered by the ENCYCLOPEDIA, we present the essential facts about the relevant biology; the symptoms, diagnosis, and treatment of common diseases and disorders; and ways in which you can prevent or reduce the severity of health problems when that is possible. The ENCYCLOPEDIA also projects what may lie ahead in the way of future treatment or prevention strategies.

The broad range of topics and issues covered in the ENCYCLOPEDIA reflects the fact that human health encompasses physical, psychological, social, environmental, and spiritual well-being. Just as the mind and the body are inextricably linked, so, too, is the individual an integral part of the wider world that comprises his or her family, society, and environment. To discuss health in its broadest aspect it is necessary to explore the many ways in which it is connected to such fields as law, social science, public policy, economics, and even religion. And so, the ENCYCLOPEDIA is meant to be a bridge between science, medical technology, the world at large, and you. I hope that it will inspire you to pursue in greater depth particular areas of interest, and that you will take advantage of the suggestions for further reading and the lists of resources and organizations that can provide additional information.

• • • •

CHAPTER 1

ALZHEIMER'S: THE DISEASE OF THE CENTURY

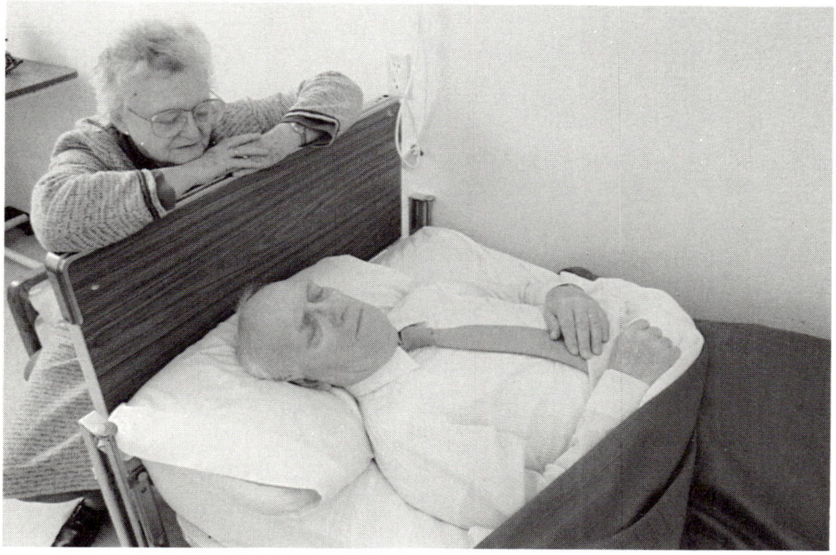

Tom was 14 years old the first time he noticed that something was wrong with his grandfather. It was during one of the frequent Sunday afternoons that his grandparents spent with Tom's family. As they were about to go in to dinner, his grandfather hesitated a second, then turned toward the outside door.

"Where are you going?" Tom's grandmother asked sharply.

The old man looked puzzled, then followed the rest of the family into the dining room, muttering something about how he had thought the dining room was in the other direction. Tom wondered what was going on, but none of the adults explained it to him, so he did not say anything.

The next time his grandparents arrived, Tom's grandmother was obviously upset. She immediately took Tom's mother, her daughter, into the kitchen for an urgent, whispered talk. Tom and his father talked with Granddad, who seemed OK, other than being a bit upset himself.

Later, after his grandparents had left, Tom's mother told his dad that Granddad had stopped the car on the way over and exclaimed to Grandma, "I hope you know where we are, because this route looks totally strange to me." Imagine! After he had driven from his house to Tom's house a hundred times or more! Tom's father attributed the lapse to "senility." After all, he pointed out, Grandfather was 71 years old. Tom's mother was not so sure. She started to talk about a visit to the doctor.

Eventually, Granddad did go to a doctor, and Tom and his family found out that he was suffering from a condition called Alzheimer's disease, an illness of the brain that insidiously and steadily robs a person of his or her mental powers. Tom's grandfather's first problem was forgetting familiar places. But in other people the first signs of Alzheimer's can be different. For instance, one woman lost the ability to form meaningful sentences. If she tried to describe her former job, she might say, "And then we, well you know those things, you know like this big, we would put them over there because, well, you know." And one can imagine a man's dismay when his elderly mother called him in an agitated condition from her home in another state and complained that the neighbors were stealing things from her home and replacing them with identical but inferior objects.

These early symptoms may seem eccentric but largely harmless and even somewhat amusing. As Alzheimer's disease inexorably progresses, however, the victim's behavior becomes bizarre, tragic, and even dangerous. It can be emotionally upsetting and exhausting to those who care for the afflicted person. One woman's mother, unable to orient herself in her daughter's house, often climbed into the shower with her daughter so as to know where she was at all times. Another victim of Alzheimer's disease, who was living with her daughter, began complaining that her son-in-law had raped her and gotten her pregnant. Still another spilled boiling water on herself, then blamed it on her grandchildren, who were not even in the city at the time. This same woman accused her daughter of being evil, and periodically called the police because she believed an old friend was trying to kill her. Sad and weary, the daughter said of her mother, "I don't know her anymore."

This type of behavior has a harmful impact on everyone in the family. One seven-year-old child wrote: "My grandfather has Alzheimer's disease. Grandpa came to stay with us. Whenever I go to eat at the table he stares at me and makes me feel like I'm going to be in trouble. He bosses me around, and I don't know what he wants. I know he doesn't know what to say, and he can't help it. I still love my Grandpa, but I wish I had a regular grandpa."

Persons with Alzheimer's disease often make constant demands and ask incessant questions in an effort to understand where and who they are and what is happening to them. The wife of one man who has Alzheimer's likens herself to a rat in a maze, where the bell is her husband's voice constantly asking, Will you help me?

The disease is in fact especially hard on the victim's spouse, who sees the couple's shared dream of a happy retirement—their golden years—disappearing. As one man wrote, "I was angry that our vision of a happy and meaningful old age was being destroyed. I knew that as long as my wife lived I would have to live with the burden of watching her die slowly—a mental death."

The victim is not spared this measure of grief. In the early stages of the disease, the Alzheimer's patient is aware that he or she is behaving strangely and can become very frightened and upset by this. In their book about Alzheimer's disease, *The Loss of Self*, Donna Cohen and Carl Eisdorfer quote this statement from a victim of the disease: "No theory of medicine can explain what is happening to me. Every few months I sense that another piece of me is missing. . . . Most people expect to die someday, but who ever expected to lose their self first?"

Perhaps the most poignant commentary on the impact of Alzheimer's disease came from the daughter of former chairman of Group W cable-television stations Donald McGannon, who said that her father had lost "the thing that was greatest about him, his mind."

The problem encountered by all these people, having to cope with a relative who has Alzheimer's disease, is an increasingly common one in the United States. One doctor has called Alzheimer's "the disease of the century." This view is justifiable when one considers it was not until the 20th century that Alzheimer's disease was recognized as a distinct illness. Still more important, it is apparent that this brain disorder will become increasingly prevalent as the century progresses. It is now 10 times more frequent than it was at the beginning of the century, and by the year 2000, the number of cases of Alzheimer's disease will increase by an additional 60%. The reason for this increasing frequency of Alzheimer's disease is that, quite simply, people are living longer. According to the Census Bureau, the percentage of elderly people (aged 65 or older) in the American population will rise from 11% in 1960 to 15% in 1990 and to 18% in the year 2020. In addition, people aged 85 years or older constitute the fastest-growing age group in the United States.

The Census Bureau estimates that 5.1 million Americans will be 85 or older by the year 2000, compared with 365,000 in that age category in 1940 and 2.5 million in 1982.

These facts are important because 9 out of every 10 victims of Alzheimer's disease are past the age of 65. The disorder occurs in about 1% of all persons between the ages of 65 and 74 years, and 7% of those 75 to 84 years of age have Alzheimer's. Finally, an astounding 25% of persons who are 85 years of age or older are victims of the disease. Combine the increased frequency of Alzheimer's disease as people get older with the longer life span of people alive today, and the result is a growing public-health problem. Officials estimate that the incidence of Alzheimer's disease in the American population will more than triple by the year 2034. Health experts predict that if no advances in treatment or prevention of the disease are made, in the year 2040 there will be 7.4 million Americans with dementia—most of them victims of Alzheimer's disease—and that half the American population will suffer dementia before they die.

Debility Is Not Inevitable

To be sure, deterioration and aging are not necessarily synonymous. Because many people still carry erroneous notions about the inevitable deterioration of mental powers in old age, it is worthwhile to briefly discuss normal aging. In the past, Alzheimer's disease, and senility generally, were thought of as part of the normal aging process. But as people live longer, more of them are aging without losing their mental faculties or talents. Examples of public figures who remained vigorous into old age (and even until the time of their death) include the actress Mae West (88), the anthropologist Margaret Mead (77), the cellist Pablo Casals (97), the painter Pablo Picasso (91), the conductor Arturo Toscanini (89), the jazz musician Duke Ellington (75), the novelist Rebecca West (91), the ragtime pianist Eubie Blake (91), and the German statesman Konrad Adenauer (91).

Ronald Reagan served 2 terms as president of the United States between the ages of 69 and 77 years. In 1981, at the age of 85, American composer Roger Sessions wrote a concerto for orchestra to commemorate the 100th anniversary of the Boston Symphony.

Norman Rockwell, one of America's most beloved artists, suffered from Alzheimer's. He died in 1978.

Group W cable television stations chairman Donald McGannon (right), who later was stricken with Alzheimer's disease, received this award from the National Association of Broadcasters in 1964.

In fact, about one-third of all people reaching age 80 or older are mentally vigorous. Another one-third display some harmless forgetfulness, and one-third are demented.

No One Is Immune

Alzheimer's disease strikes people of both sexes, and every race and income level. Among persons who have died of this disorder are the actress Rita Hayworth, the film director Otto Preminger, the illustrator Norman Rockwell, the writer E. B. White, and the mystery writer Ross McDonald. Nonetheless, as we have noted, most victims of Alzheimer's are more than 65 years old.

We can see from the story of Tom and his grandfather told at the beginning of this chapter how young people may also be affected by the presence of Alzheimer's. Many already have or will have a relative who develops the disease as that relative grows older. Most of us know very little about Alzheimer's, and what we know is often incorrect. It will be helpful to have an accurate body of knowledge in coping with a relative who has the disease.

Learning the current facts about Alzheimer's disease will also enable you to add new information about the disease to what you already know, as more is discovered about Alzheimer's disease in the near future. There will probably be no "magic cures" for Alzheimer's disease. But considerable time and money are being spent to understand this illness, how it is caused, and how best to care for persons who have it. There are also important legislative proposals designed to make Alzheimer's disease less of a disaster to families. You will understand these better if you know about the illness and how it affects victims and their families.

Finally, Alzheimer's disease is an extremely prevalent issue in the late 20th century. Public awareness of this disease is expanding rapidly. Dr. Lewis Thomas, former chancellor of Memorial Sloan-Kettering Cancer Center in New York City, recently said that "of all the health problems in the 20th century, this is one of the worst."

In 1984 Margaret Heckler, secretary of Health and Human Services, and Daniel Tosteson, dean of the Harvard Medical School, announced the creation of a center for the study of Alzheimer's at Harvard.

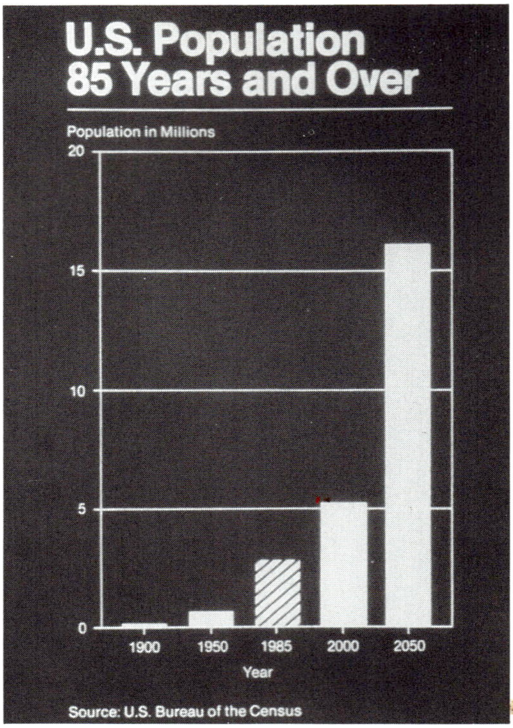

A graph from the U.S. Census Bureau illustrates that the number of Americans who are living past the age of 85 has increased dramatically since 1900, and projects that it will continue to rise in the 21st century.

Deprived of Mind

One of the most important facts about Alzheimer's disease is that even though its victims often exhibit strange, irrational, and emotionally upsetting behavior, the disease is not a psychological or mental illness. Rather, it is a physical disorder whose symptoms are caused by the death and destruction of nerve cells in very specific areas of the brain.

Alzheimer's is one of a group of diseases called *dementias*. The primary effects of any dementia—a term that literally means "deprived of mind"—are cognitive. That is, they concern the mental and intellectual faculties and the ability to learn, think, and reason. Alzheimer's disease causes a progressive loss of mental faculties, often beginning with memory, learning, attention, and judgment. In time the peson with Alzheimer's disease loses all aspects of thought, feeling, and behavior. Death eventually follows, usually from complications such as pneumonia, infection of the urinary tract, and the many other problems common to bedridden elderly patients.

About half of all Alzheimer's cases eventually result in the patient's becoming incapacitated. As a result, many people in nursing homes are there because of Alzheimer's. Some experts believe that as many as half the nation's 1.3 million nursing home residents may have Alzheimer's disease.

In one 500-bed geriatric nursing home in New York City (in which the average age of the residents was 85), Dr. Robert Katzman of the University of California, San Diego at La Jolla, and his colleagues found that 65% of the residents met the clinical and mental criteria for having dementia. In a series of 100 autopsies done on patients from this nursing home, they found evidence of Alzheimer's disease in the brains of 55 patients, or 55% of the residents of the home.

West German statesman Konrad Adenauer is surrounded by his family at his 87th birthday party in 1963. Hundreds of thousands of people remain healthy and active well into their eighties and nineties.

But even though Alzheimer's disease is the nation's fourth leading killer of older people, mortality is not the most important effect of this disease, according to a 1986 government report entitled *Losing a Million Minds*. Of equal or greater concern is the loss of autonomy caused by Alzheimer's disease, which brings on catastrophic expenses caused by the need for long-term care for its victims.

The popular physician-author Dr. William Nolen has expressed the threat of Alzheimer's disease very well. "Alzheimer's is a condition in which degenerative changes occur in the cortex, the upper level of the brain where the 'higher' functions—thinking, reasoning, remembering—are carried on," says Dr. Nolen. "That's one reason why it's so scary—it affects those very activities that make us human."

• • • •

CHAPTER 2

DISCOVERING A DISEASE

Alois Alzheimer

Alzheimer's disease was not recognized as a distinct clinical entity until relatively recently. In 1906 a German physician named Alois Alzheimer reported to a meeting of psychiatrists his observations of unusual changes in the brain of a woman who had died at the age of 55, almost 5 years after developing dementia.

Using recently developed silver stains containing silver compounds that showed more clearly the structure of brain cells,

Alzheimer demonstrated that the cerebral cortex—the seat of the brain's intellectual functions—contained abnormal nerve cells with tangles of fibers and clusters of degenerating nerve endings. Here was a clear demonstration that an apparently psychological disease could have an organic, or physical, origin. In an age when mental illnesses were poorly understood, this was a very welcome finding.

But there was an unusual feature about the case. The woman had exhibited symptoms of dementia such as memory loss, disorientation, and hallucinations. But her dementia had begun at the age of 51, which was rather young. Did the brain abnormalities in this relatively young woman also apply to cases of dementia in older persons? Alzheimer chose to interpret his case as an example of a separate illness, which he called presenile dementia, or dementia occurring before old age.

Alzheimer published his report in 1907. It immediately became the focus of controversy, which continued in some measure until the 1970s. Three critical questions were raised by this case:

1. Is presenile dementia—Alzheimer's disease—different from senile dementia—dementia occurring in a person over age 65?
2. Does arteriosclerosis—hardening of the arteries—play a major causative role in either condition?
3. Are either or both forms of dementia the inevitable accompaniment of aging?

The answer to all three questions turned out to be no.

The medical world at first resisted the idea that dementia in persons of different ages is a common occurrence. It had been an accepted tenet, since the time of the ancient Greeks, that susceptibility to disease is age related, meaning that the older a person is, the more likely he or she is to contract a given illness. But investigations of the brains of stricken persons gradually uncovered the same pattern of physical abnormalities in the brains of those with senile dementia and those with presenile (Alzheimer's) dementia, leading scientists to conclude that the two diseases are identical. Both early and late versions may be called Alzheimer's disease.

Until the late 1960s, almost anyone older than 65 who experienced marked confusion, disorientation, and memory loss was said to have arteriosclerosis of the brain, a condition that was thought an inevitable result of aging, as well as progressive and incurable. But arteriosclerosis was rejected as a major cause of dementia, primarily because of two landmark papers by Drs. Bernard E. Tomlinson, Garry Blessed, and Martin Roth in 1968 and 1970. These scientists found large amounts of fatty deposits in artery walls of the brains of both demented and healthy elderly people. Moreover, 50% of the brains of elderly people suffering from dementia did not contain arteriosclerotic lesions. Within the next five years, scientists also rejected the possibility that diseases of the blood vessels were a major cause of dementia. This meant that only a small percentage of cases of dementia could be explained by damage to the arteries in the brain. Such cases are now called *multi-infarct dementias* (see Chapter 5).

At first, physicians believed that dementia was an inevitable part of aging. But this attitude changed when a specific chemical deficit was found in the brains of Alzheimer's disease patients but not in the brains of mentally healthy aged persons (see Chapter 3). Most physicians and neuroscientists now view Alzheimer's disease as an abnormal condition completely separate from the aging process.

Symptoms and Progress

The controversy that greeted Alois Alzheimer's findings in 1907 has long since been put to rest. The existence of a disease with a specific set of symptoms, which are present in the large majority of cases and progress in a characteristic way, is no longer in question.

The first symptoms of Alzheimer's disease are typically mild and usually involve forgetfulness of minor things, such as leaving a briefcase behind or missing a dental appointment. At one time it was thought that a person with Alzheimer's disease first forgets more recent events and remembers more clearly those things that were experienced further back in time. But a 1984 study presented to the International Study Group on the Treatment of Memory Disorders Associated with Aging found that persons with the disease forget both old and new events equally.

Forgetfulness is accompanied by the inability to learn new information. A lawyer may find it impossible to retain the details of a case he or she is working on. Or one may find oneself repeatedly asking the name of someone to whom one has just been introduced.

The person who has developed Alzheimer's disease also forgets simple skills that he or she has possessed for a long time, such as tying a shoelace or telling time. A carpenter may no longer be able to saw a straight line; a secretary will start to garble phone messages. In one particularly sad case, a music teacher was no longer able to read music. All abilities are equally vulnerable to loss.

Speech is a faculty that is almost invariably affected early in Alzheimer's disease, and it degrades progressively as the disease advances. An affected person speaks "empty speech," which is grammatically correct but has no meaning; eventually, almost all persons with Alzheimer's disease produce completely meaningless sentences.

As cognitive skills deteriorate, more complex mental tasks become impossible. Doing arithmetic sums is beyond the ability of many persons with moderately advanced Alzheimer's disease. Such persons also no longer understand the point of cartoons. Soon, common sense and judgment disappear: For instance, a person whose illness is in the early or moderately advanced stages may dress for winter in midsummer. The disorientation caused by the disease may in some cases be dangerous, as when an Alzheimer's victim loses his or her bearings in open and public places. Those people are sometimes found wandering along a road or highway or walking about their home or neighborhood in the middle of the night. They also become disoriented with regard to time, sometimes slipping back mentally into childhood. Often, they fail to recognize loved ones or friends.

Some persons may exhibit bizarre, apparently inexplicable behavior as the first sign of Alzheimer's disease. The wife of one man with the disease told *Time* magazine that she was confused about why rags were mysteriously collecting in the family car: "I couldn't figure out what Tony was doing with these rags. . . . It turned out he knew how to start the car and how to drive, but he couldn't figure out how to use the windshield wipers or defroster any more." Another patient was picked up for shoplifting in a grocery store. In both cases their abnormal behavior was the first clear manifestation that something was wrong.

During the course of the disease, many Alzheimer's patients have difficulty controlling their bodies and extremities. These difficulties signal degeneration of the various parts of the brain that control the muscles. The individual affected may have trouble in moving an arm or leg, which is often held rigidly; or he or she may be able to move only slowly or with a tremor. These are the same symptoms exhibited by persons with Parkinson's disease, and it is therefore not surprising that some of the brain abnormalities seen in the latter illness are the same as those found in the brain in many cases of Alzheimer's disease.

Another common symptom of Alzheimer's disease is emotional disturbance. Early in the course of their dementia, persons frequently can sense that their intellectual function is failing. This can lead them to profound depression and withdrawal, further limiting their intellectual capacity. They may also have crying spells or temper tantrums at their inability to do tasks that were once simple for them.

As Alzheimer's disease advances into its more severe stages, the victim begins to demonstrate more disturbing signs of change in the emotions and behavior. The individual tends to withdraw

During the course of Alzheimer's disease patients may have difficulty controlling their muscles, so that simple tasks such as holding a ball become difficult and sometimes impossible.

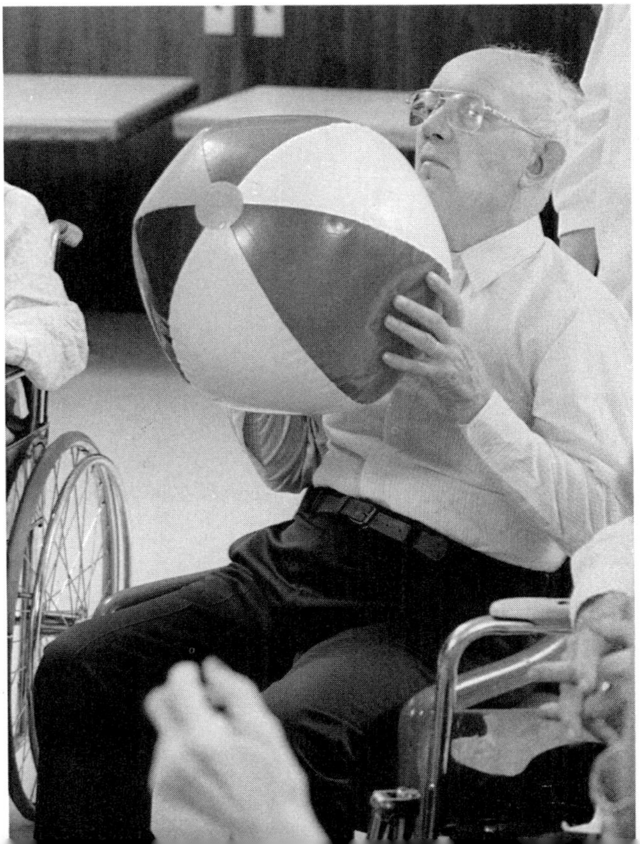

from all social contact. Some afflicted persons become paranoid, believing that their family is plotting to take away their property or to put them away in an institution. Irritability, agitation, anxiety, and even verbal and physical aggression toward family members may develop, particularly as the dementia progresses and the victim feels an increasing loss of control over his or her environment.

In the final stages of Alzheimer's disease, those affected by it become apathetic, disoriented, and oblivious to other people's reactions. They may also become incontinent during this phase. Some lose their ability to walk and may develop contractures of the face, arms, and legs, ending up curled into a fetal position.

The relentless course of Alzheimer's disease carries with it a sentence of eventual mental emptiness. But for different individuals it takes different periods of time to reach this final stage of dementia, from as little as 10 months after the onset of the disease to as long as 10 years. Although predicting the course of Alzheimer's disease is almost impossible, there is some evidence that those in whom the disease has its onset earlier in life (during their forties and fifties) lose their cognitive faculties more rapidly. On the average, victims of Alzheimer's disease die between 7 and 10 years after the onset of the illness.

• • • •

CHAPTER 3

ALZHEIMER'S AND THE BRAIN

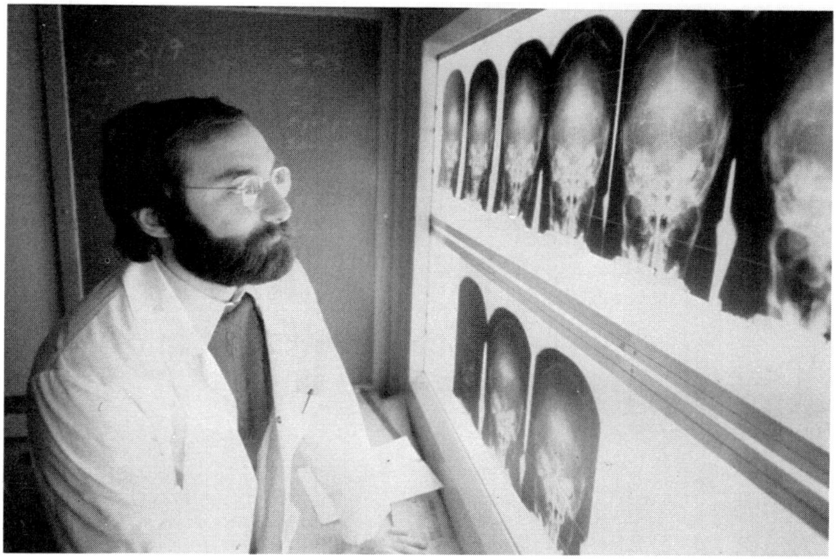

The pioneering techniques of Alois Alzheimer and his colleagues initiated what has become a continuing investigation of the brains of persons with Alzheimer's disease. Modern neuropathologists, doctors who study abnormalities of the nervous system, including brain tissue, use the latest biochemical stains, electron microscopes, and techniques of molecular analysis to uncover fundamental changes in the brains of victims of the disease.

Our understanding of the link between brain abnormalities and Alzheimer's disease is rapidly increasing. However, the two deviations from the norm in brain physiology discovered by Alois Alzheimer in 1906—the tangles of protein fibrils and patches of abnormal protein called plaques—remain the hallmarks of the disease and the focus of intense research efforts.

Brain Abnormalities in Alzheimer's Victims

The following is a compendium of the most prominent abnormalities found in the brains of persons suffering from Alzheimer's disease, ranging from the most severe to the most minor.

Loss of Nerve Cells from the Cerebral Cortex: The cerebral cortex is the seat of memory and thought. Alzheimer's disease reduces the number of neurons in this region by about 10%. Even when the disease has progressed to its most severe stage, and the patient has ceased to talk and needs help with the activities of daily living, nerve-cell loss in the brain does not become measurably greater than this. A 10% loss is relatively minor and probably cannot account for the severe cognitive impairment seen in Alzheimer's disease.

Neurofibrillary Tangles: These are unusual groups of neurofibrils, which are normal structural elements of nerve cells. The neurofibrillary tangles in Alzheimer's disease are found within the cell bodies of nerve cells in the cerebral cortex. These fibers have adopted the highly abnormal form of a paired helix in which two strands are wound around one another. Similar structures are also found (although not as extensively) in the brains of persons with postencephalitic Parkinson's disease (encephalitis is an inflammation of the brain caused by a viral infection), adults with Down's syndrome (a form of mental subnormality due to a chromosome defect), and former prizefighters suffering from *dementia pugilistica,* or "punch-drunk" syndrome (a result of damage to the brain from repeated trauma). It is difficult to imagine what these three conditions, with their very different etiologies, or origins, can have in common that causes these bizarre tangles in each case.

Neuritic Plaques: These are patches of clumped material lying outside the bodies of nerve cells in the brain. They are found chiefly in the cerebral cortex but also in other areas of the brain. At the core of each plaque is a substance called amyloid, an abnormal protein not usually found in the brain. This amyloid core is surrounded by cast-off fragments of dead or dying nerve cells. These cell fragments include dying mitochondria (the "energy factories" that living cells use to produce the energy that drives their various functions), incomplete presynaptic terminals (the contact points between nerve cells), and paired helical filaments identical to those that constitute the neurofibrillary tangles. In the eyes of some neuropathologists, the plaques found in the brains of persons with Alzheimer's disease are essentially clusters of degenerating nerve terminals. A major question about these plaques is how and why have these fragments clustered together?

Congophilic Angiopathy: This is the technical name that neuropathologists have given to an abnormality found in the walls of blood vessels in the brains of victims of Alzheimer's disease. (*Congophilic* refers to the change of color in the blood-vessel walls when they are exposed to a stain called Congo red.) These abnormal patches are similar to the neuritic plaques that develop in Alzheimer's disease, in that amyloid has been found within the blood-vessel walls wherever the patches occur. Another name for these patches is *cerebrovascular amyloid,* meaning amyloid found in the blood vessels of the brain.

Hirano Bodies: These structural abnormalities were first observed by a neuropathologist in 1968 in the brains of persons with an unusual form of dementia found among Indian natives of the Pacific island of Guam. Subsequently, they were also found in the brains of persons who had died with Alzheimer's dementia. Actin, another major structural protein of the living cell, is the major component of Hirano bodies. In the late 1970s, scientists found that Hirano bodies contain ribosomes, the structures within the cell that translate the genetic messages encoded in the nucleic acids of all living cells into proteins that make up the components and vital contents of the cell. But the ribosomes in Hirano bodies are in a dormant form and cannot accomplish this step of translating the genetic message into proteins—a defect that may inhibit the formation of memory. Like most other structural abnormalities in Alzheimer's disease, Hirano bodies are found mainly in the hippocampus, the region of the cerebral cortex that plays an essential role in memory processing.

Large declines in the enzyme responsible for the formation of the chemical messenger acetylcholine: Acetylcholine is a substance that carries signals from one nerve cell to another. It is known to be important to learning and memory. For instance, in the early 1970s, two neuroscientists gave healthy young volunteers the drug scopolamine, which blocks the action of acetylcholine. The subjects temporarily suffered a striking impairment of their ability to retain new information that was presented to them, and to recall old information that they had known for some time.

In the mid-1970s, scientists found that the brains of persons afflicted by Alzheimer's disease contained 60 to 90% less of the enzyme choline acetyltransferase (CAT)—which is responsible for producing acetylcholine—than did the brains of healthy persons. This was particularly true in the cerebral cortex and hippocampus. Finding this decreased quantity of CAT was an important milestone. All abnormalities previously found in the brains of persons with the disease were structural; the decline in CAT is a functional change directly related to learning and memory.

Decreased levels of the chemical messenger somatostatin: The substance known as somatostatin is another means by which cells in the brain communicate with each other. The quantities of this chemical messenger, like those of CAT, are also greatly decreased in the cerebral cortex and the hippocampus of persons

A microphotograph of neurons. Alzheimer's disease patients may suffer as much as a 10% loss of neurons in the cerebral cortex, the area of the brain concerned with memory and thought.

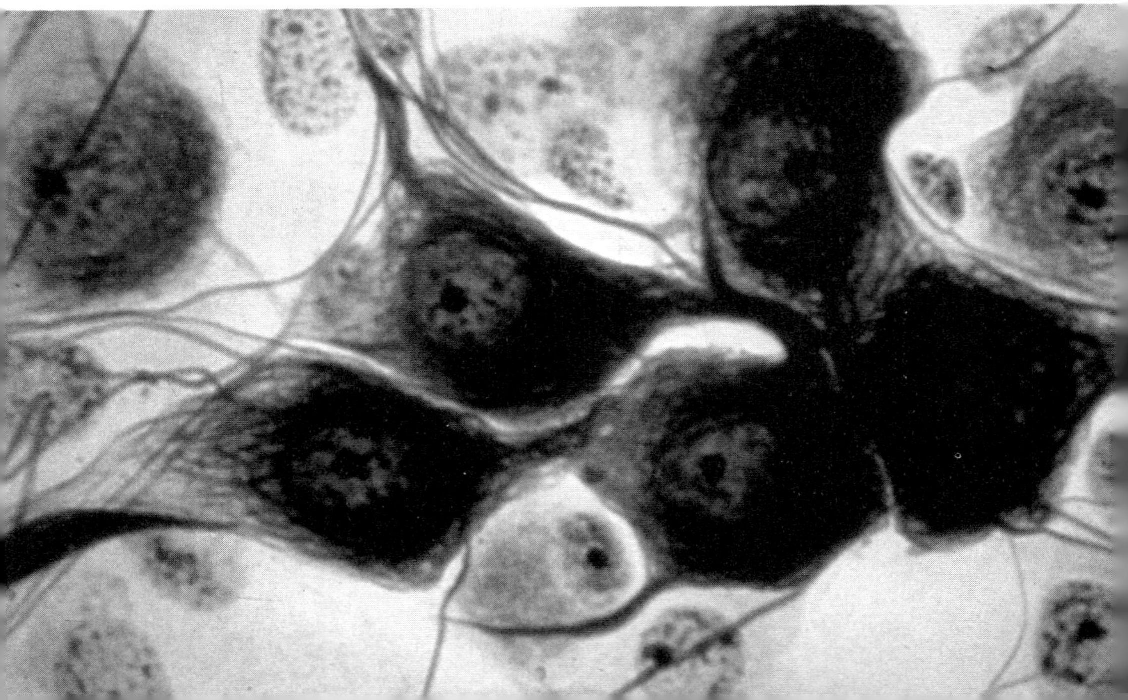

with Alzheimer's disease. In fact, somatostatin is lost to almost the same degree as is CAT. A few other brain chemicals, in addition to CAT and somatostatin, are present in abnormally low quantities in the brains of persons with Alzheimer's disease, although most are found in normal quantities.

A striking loss of the neurons that transmit CAT-containing processes to the cortex: Once scientists realized that loss of the power to manufacture acetylcholine is a major deficit in the brains of persons with Alzheimer's disease, they set out to discover why this loss occurs. They discovered that the loss of CAT occurs in the cortex. But nerve cells characteristically send out long, thin extensions, or processes, that make contact with other nerve cells in distant areas of the brain, just as long-distance telephone lines permit messages to be transmitted to faraway places. CAT is found at the very ends of these long processes. But although they were able to find these long, CAT-containing processes, scientists could not find the cell bodies that sent out these processes to the cortex—the "telephones" from which the long transmission lines originated. They postulated that the death of these cells may be the primary form of brain damage in Alzheimer's disease.

Plaques and Tangles

Several studies with primates and other mammals whose brains are structured much like those of humans revealed a previously ignored region called the nucleus basalis of Meynert (nbM), or *basal nucleus,* as the largest concentration of neurons that use acetylcholine to transmit messages to the cortex of the brain. The basal nucleus is a small area located deep within the brain, in a largely unexplored region called the *substantia innominata*—the "unnamed material." When scientists examined the nbM in the brains of victims of Alzheimer's disease, they hit the jackpot: Striking numbers of neurons had disappeared from the nbM in every case. This landmark discovery was made only in the early 1980s and represents a major neuropathological discovery in the investigation of Alzheimer's disease. Many scientists believe that this discovery explains why the plaques in Alzheimer's disease resemble clusters of degenerating nerve terminals: They may well consist of dying and disintegrating processes from the missing neurons in the basal nucleus.

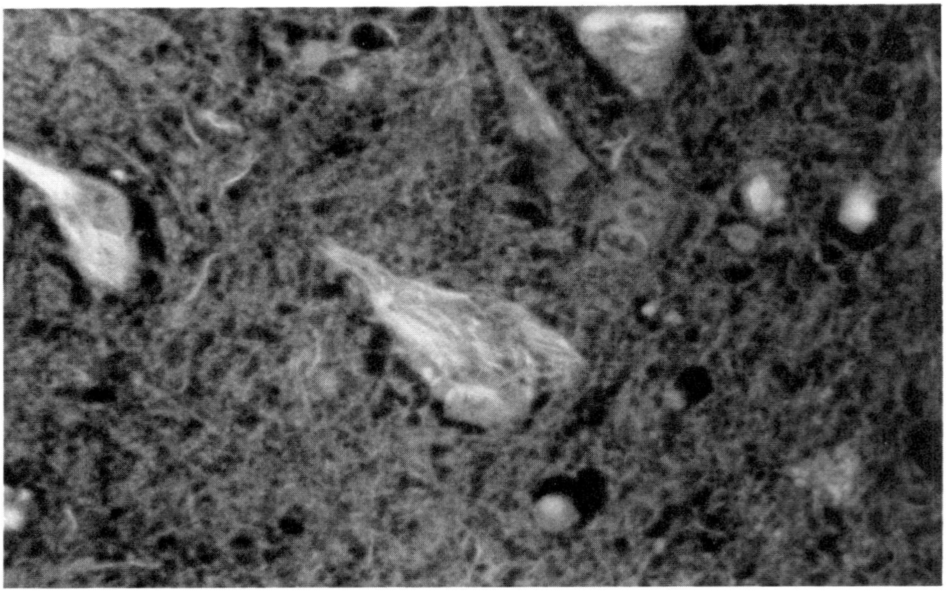

Neurofibrillary tangles, which occur in the cerebral cortex of Alzheimer's victims, have also been found in people with postencephalitic Parkinson's disease and in adults with Down's syndrome.

Another interesting fact that scientists discovered is that virtually all of the changes characteristic of Alzheimer's disease are also seen, although to a lesser degree, in the brains of elderly persons who do not have the disease. This discovery does not make it less likely that the loss of CAT and death of neurons in the basal nucleus are important in causing Alzheimer's disease. Rather, it probably means that Alzheimer's disease is a threshold phenomenon, which occurs when cell death exceeds a certain limit or threshold, rather than being a "unique condition" that suddenly affects the brain.

Furthermore, the extent to which the cognitive function of the brain is disturbed in Alzheimer's disease is directly related to the extent of the structural damage and disturbance in the brains of persons who have the disease. Evidence of this was found in 1968, when epidemiologists in Great Britain examined the clinical records of 104 aged persons who had died, and autopsied their brains. In an important study, they concluded that the more plaques and tangles an individual has, the greater his or her cognitive loss. In Switzerland in 1981, another research team found that the more extensive the concentration of plaques and tangles in the hippocampus and the cortex, the greater was the memory loss that an individual experienced. In a study of nearly 650 elderly Swiss patients, 100% of those who had very extensive brain abnormalities suffered from amnesia, as compared to 30% of those with no noticeable brain lesions. There is also a strong correlation between changes in the scores on mental-status examinations of elderly persons and the loss of choline acetyltransferase from their brain. Because of this, scientists have concluded that the brain lesions that occur in Alzheimer's disease are directly related to the loss of mental functioning experienced by patients with the disease. Current research is therefore focused on trying to understand how plaques and tangles might form in the brains of persons with Alzheimer's disease. Because plaques and tangles appear to be the result of the death of cells in the basal nucleus, another line of inquiry is to look for possible causes of the death of those cells.

In 1985 and 1986, scientists isolated the major amyloid proteins from the plaques, neurofibrillary tangles, and cerebrovascular amyloid deposits in the brains of persons with Alzheimer's disease. They determined the compositions of these proteins. The

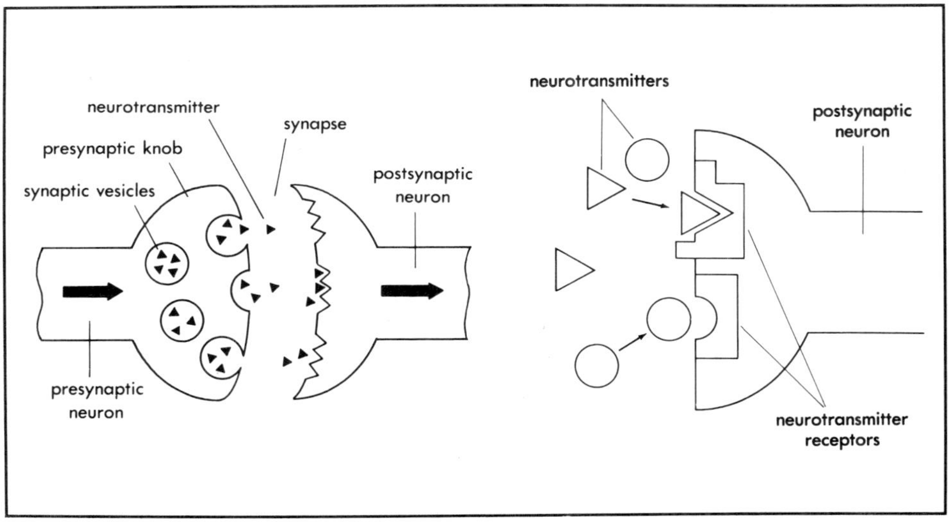

Left: *One neuron signals another by emitting a neurotransmitter such as acetylcholine—crucial to memory and learning—across a synapse.* Right: *Each neurotransmitter fits one kind of receptor on the target neuron.*

sequences in which the amino acids of the proteins were joined together were very different from those of any known amyloid proteins, and, in fact, were different from those of any protein whose amino acid composition had previously been determined.

Dr. Robert Katzman of the University of California, San Diego, has offered an explanation for how amyloid proteins may contribute to the formation of the bizarre structures found in the brains of persons with Alzheimer's disease. He suggests that amyloid proteins are made in diseased neurons, such as those in the nbM. Within these diseased nerve cells, amyloid proteins form paired helical filaments, which accumulate to form neurofibrillary tangles. Some helical filaments are carried along the thin, extended processes that project from the cell body of the nerve cell until they reach nerve terminals. Here, the amyloid proteins are squeezed out of the nerve cell, or perhaps released when the cell dies and breaks apart, and become part of the neuritic plaques found in the brains of persons with Alzheimer's disease. The amyloid proteins are then taken up by blood vessels, in which they form the patches of cerebrovascular amyloid that are also generated by this disease.

Dr. Katzman says that this idea was actually suggested 60 years ago but was ignored. It has been revived by the recent molecular studies of amyloid proteins in Alzheimer's disease.

In November 1986, a group of scientists announced that they had found, in the chromosomes from three patients with Alzheimer's disease, multiple copies of a gene that makes one type of amyloid protein. They suggested that the presence of multiple copies of this gene within each cell might lead to the overproduction of amyloid protein, which could explain why the amyloid proteins in the brains of patients with Alzheimer's disease aggregated into strange structures. However, this idea was later discounted, as has been the case with so many hopeful claims made about Alzheimer's disease. Neither the original research group nor two others were able to find more than one set of amyloid genes in the patients they studied.

In March 1987, several research teams simultaneously reported a less spectacular finding in the drive to understand the role of amyloid protein in Alzheimer's disease. They isolated the gene that makes amyloid—a step that will promote basic research in the production of amyloid protein in living cells.

In another important step, scientists announced in November 1986 that they had discovered an additional abnormal protein present only in the brains of deceased victims of Alzheimer's disease or in the spinal fluid of those afflicted and still living. A group of scientists led by Dr. Peter Davies, of the Albert Einstein College of Medicine in New York City, named this new protein A68. In 1987 they also found A68 in the brains of normal infants, where it persists until two years of age. Dr. Davies and his co-workers reported that the A68 protein is 1,000 times more abundant in the brains of persons with Alzheimer's disease than in the brains of infants. However, many questions about A68 remain to be answered. For example, it has not yet been definitely proven that A68 is different from the amyloid proteins. There is also the question of what role the A68 protein has, if any, in the formation of the plaques and neurofibrillary tangles typical of Alzheimer's disease. One suggestion is that A68 appears in cells that are destined to die. It is known that many of the neurons in the brains of newborn infants die during the first few years of life, and the A68 protein may play some part in this cell death.

A branch of the National Institutes of Health has established two centers for the study of the brains of deceased Alzheimer's victims.

Answers Through Autopsy

Most of what has been learned so far about the dementias, from the observations of Alois Alzheimer in 1906 to the finding that neurons are lost from the basal nucleus of the brain in 1982, has come from the postmortem study of brain tissue. Two brain banks set up by the National Institute of Neurological and Communicative Diseases and Stroke—a unit of the National Institutes of Health—have enhanced the study of brains from deceased victims of Alzheimer's disease. These banks work closely with voluntary health organizations and have set up simple procedures to make it easy for families of victims of Alzheimer's to donate tissue to the banks.

The importance of obtaining permission for autopsies from spouses or relatives of deceased Alzheimer's victims cannot be overstated. However, some doctors believe that as the public becomes more aware of the disease and develops an interest in contributing to research into its causes, possible treatments, and preventive measures, obtaining such permission will become easier.

• • • •

CHAPTER 4

POSSIBLE CAUSES OF ALZHEIMER'S

Seeking the cause of Alzheimer's disease has been a baffling exercise for scientists. For most of this century, very little was known about the specific damage that it does to the brains of its victims. Now that scientists know more about the special nerve-cell pathways that are destroyed in the course of the disease, more incisive research can begin on the cause of cell death. Four hypotheses have been developed that can serve as starting points for investigations into the origin of Alzheimer's disease. Attention has focused on kuru and Creutzfeldt-Jakob disease because the brains of their victims show nerve-cell death as well as plaques containing amyloidlike material.

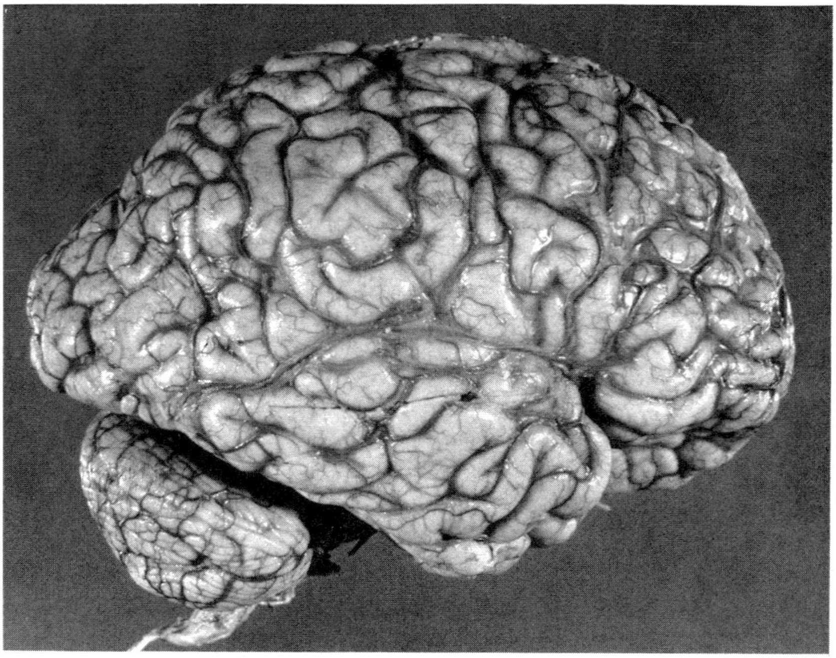

Scientists have made strides in determining what causes Alzheimer's by studying the brains of both normal (above) and diseased persons.

Viral Links

It has been proposed that Alzheimer's disease is caused by the selective death of brain cells as a result of viral infection. This explanation was suggested by two other diseases in which the destruction of brain cells leads to deterioration of the mental function: the relatively rare kuru and Creutzfeldt-Jakob disease. They are viral infections, an overabundance of aluminum and other toxins, and possibly the breakdown of the immune system. Based on the patterns in which these two diseases are transmitted, scientists hypothesize that both diseases are provoked by viruses, although they have not actually been able to isolate the virus in either case. Kuru, a fatal and rapidly progressive neurological illness, was found among primitive tribes in New Guinea and was spread by cannibalism. Although no virus has been found in Creutzfeldt-Jakob disease, this condition is known to be infectious and much like Alzheimer's disease, is marked by premature dementia and loss of muscle control.

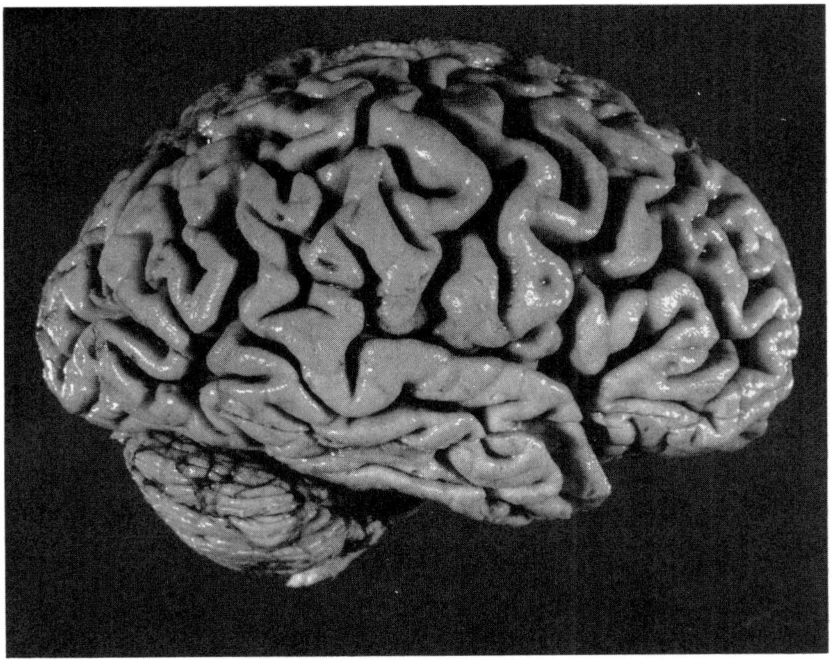

A photograph of the brain of an Alzheimer's disease victim. Note the substantial sulci, or widened valleys, on the surface of the brain.

Investigators at the National Institutes of Health (NIH) have attempted to detect the presence of a virus in the brains of Alzheimer's disease patients. They took tissue samples from the brains of persons who had died from the disease and placed them in laboratory dishes with growing cells. In some cases, the brain extracts seemed to cause the cell cultures to die.

In other experiments, the brain extracts were injected into chimpanzees. After two to three years, two of six chimps that were injected with this material developed a progressive neurological illness. This long time lag was not surprising. The viruses that cause kuru and Creutzfeldt-Jakob disease also take a long time to produce symptoms and in fact belong to a family of viruses called the "slow viruses.") Unfortunately, neither the investigators at the NIH nor any others who performed similar experiments were able to reproduce these results. At present, the hypothesis of a viral cause for Alzheimer's disease is a question mark.

A New Guinea tribe. The cannabilistic practices of such tribes once transmitted a brain virus with symptoms similar to those of Alzheimer's.

An even more unusual hypothesis for the origin of Alzheimer's disease has been advanced by Dr. Stanley Prusiner of the University of California, San Francisco. Dr. Prusiner has proposed that the disease is caused by viruslike particles called prions. These mysterious particles have been found in other brain diseases, such as rabies. And some scientists believe that prionlike substances are present in the brains of victims of Alzheimer's disease. However, the particles are very difficult to grow and work with, making it difficult to draw firm conclusions about any role they may have in Alzheimer's disease.

Most scientists are still skeptical about the role of prions in the illness. In an editorial published in *The New England Journal of Medicine* on December 17, 1987, Dr. Bernard N. Fields of the Harvard Medical School said that suggestions about prions as a cause of aging, Alzheimer's disease, or disease of the pancreas, as well as their relevance to any other degenerative diseases, are "so speculative that they belong largely to the realm of science fiction."

Aluminum and Other Toxins

A second hypothesis regarding the cause of Alzheimer's disease has attempted to link the disease to the excessive accumulation of aluminum or other toxic materials in brain cells. The so-called aluminum intoxication theory of Alzheimer's disease has been supported by several suggestive findings. Unfortunately, none of them have been free of contradictory findings.

Initial suspicion about a toxic cause for Alzheimer's disease focused on aluminum because of dementia in patients who were on kidney dialysis. It was found that aluminum in both the blood-cleansing fluid and in the antacids used for dialysis patients produced significant concentrations of aluminum in the blood of these patients. As a result, aluminum collected in the patients' brain, leading to the death of brain cells. This finding, in the early 1970s, led scientists to ask whether the brain damage that occurs in persons with Alzheimer's disease might not be caused by an accumulation of aluminum in their brain.

A worker cuts ribbons of aluminum. One hypothesis about the cause of Alzheimer's is that the disease is linked to an excessive accumulation of aluminum or other toxic materials in brain cells.

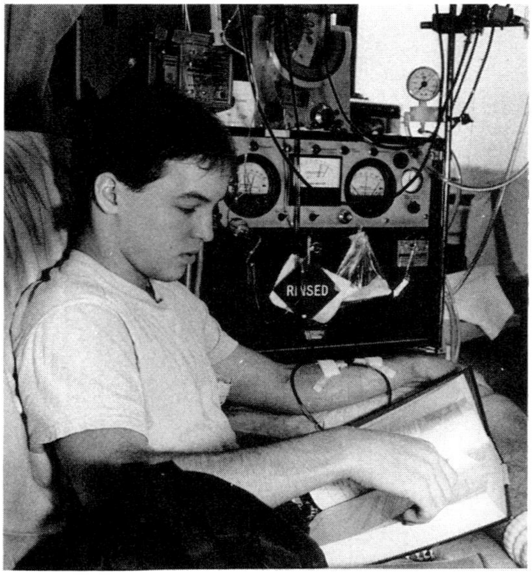

A teenager on kidney dialysis. Research reveals that the antacids used on dialysis patients can cause an excessive amount of aluminum in the blood, sometimes accompanied by dementia. This finding led scientists to explore the possibility of a connection between aluminum accumulation and Alzheimer's disease.

There is evidence that the aluminum content of the normal brain increases during aging. An additional increase in the aluminum content of the brains of Alzheimer's disease patients was suggested by autopsy investigations at the University of Toronto in the early 1970s. These studies showed that the brains of affected individuals contain as much as 30 times more aluminum than the brains of healthy persons of the same age.

However, researchers at the University of Kentucky did not find increased amounts of aluminum in brains of persons with Alzheimer's disease. This was a crucial test, because the Kentucky natives whom the researchers studied had drunk water with a high aluminum content all their lives, and if increased aluminum concentrations could be found in the brains of the Alzheimer's patients anywhere, they should have been found in Kentucky.

Scientists have attempted to clarify the role of aluminum in Alzheimer's disease by treating animals with this mineral. The injection of aluminum salts into animals, either into the animal's veins or directly into their brains, has produced changes in the brain somewhat like the abnormalities seen in Alzheimer's disease. But the tangles seen in the animals' brains are different from those seen in humans with Alzheimer's disease.

The situation has been made even more complex by the discovery of increased quantities of silicon in the brains of Alzheimer's patients. Most recently, scientists reported in 1986 that they found aluminum silicate in amyloid plaques in the brains of those suffering from the disorder. How can the brain form this compound? And what is it doing there?

So far, research on the presence of aluminum in brains of persons afflicted by Alzheimer's has provided more questions than answers. One possibility is that accumulations of aluminum within damaged brain cells may be a consequence of nerve cell damage, rather than a cause of it.

Genetics

Is Alzheimer's disease caused by a genetic defect, or is there at least a genetic tendency to develop the disease? The search for a genetic basis of Alzheimer's disease is at this time the most active area of research into this illness. Several facts suggest that the disease may have a genetic component. For one thing, "clusters" of Alzheimer's cases have been reported within families. In these families, if a parent has the disease, the children have a 50% chance of developing it. Generally, these cases, which are called familial Alzheimer's disease (or FAD), are more severe and typically demonstrate an early onset (between the ages of 40 and 50) and a more rapid progression. They are exaggerated versions of the more typical, nonfamilial form of Alzheimer's, which accounts for 90% of all cases.

But even without FAD, there is an increased risk that the close relatives of a patient with Alzheimer's will eventually develop the disease. The general probability of getting the disease is between 2 and 3%; if a parent or brother or sister is already afflicted, the likelihood of another member of the immediate family falling ill with Alzheimer's disease increases to between 7 and 8%. Dr. Leonard Heston of the University of Minnesota found a familial link in about one-third of the 144 families he has studied that include an Alzheimer's disease patient. This familial component is age related: The earlier the age at which a person gets the disease, the greater is the risk that other members of the person's family will also develop it. If the disease is diagnosed in a parent over the age of 70, the risk to the parent's children increases only very slightly.

In addition, there is a puzzling connection between Alzheimer's disease and Down's syndrome. The latter condition, in which a child is born mentally retarded, is caused by an abnormality in the child's chromosomes, the carriers of heredity. Normally, each person has 46 chromosomes, that is, 2 copies of each of 23 different chromosomes. One set of 23 chromosomes is inherited from the mother, the other set from the father. In Down's syndrome there are three copies of one of the chromosomes, chromosome 21. Apparently, having an extra chromosome can be as damaging as not having a full set.

Several phenomena connect Alzheimer's disease and Down's syndrome. First, persons with Down's syndrome who survive beyond the age of 40 (an increasingly common occurrence these days) experience brain changes similar to those seen in Alzheimer's disease.

Second, the frequency of Down's syndrome is 10 times greater among families of persons who have early-onset Alzheimer's disease. Third, close relatives of both Alzheimer's patients and Down's syndrome patients have an increased chance of developing blood and lymph cancers, such as Hodgkin's disease and some leukemias.

Because the cause of Down's syndrome—the extra copy of chromosome number 21—is so specific, it is a likely source at which to start looking for a genetic component of Alzheimer's disease. In early 1987, a team of scientists at the Massachusetts General Hospital in Boston reported finding a stretch of genetic material on chromosome 21 that is linked to the appearance of the familial form of Alzheimer's disease (FAD). There are approximately 500 genes on this segment of the chromosome, and one or more of them is thought to cause the familial form of Alzheimer's disease. Because scientists believe that FAD and the more common, sporadic form of Alzheimer's disease are related to the same gene(s), studying this section of chromosome 21 may shed light on all cases of the disorder.

As exciting as these genetic discoveries about Alzheimer's disease are, Dr. Katzman points out that genetics is at best only part of the Alzheimer's disease story. For instance, Alzheimer's does not always occur simultaneously in identical twins and may occur in one twin whereas the second never develops the illness. There is a report of one set of twins who both developed Alzheimer's disease—but 13 years apart.

A boy with Down's syndrome. Studies show that people with this genetic defect who survive past the age of 40 experience brain changes that are similar to those of Alzheimer's disease patients.

The Immune System and the Death of Brain Cells

The fourth working hypothesis proposed as a cause of Alzheimer's disease speculates that it is the result of an age-related change in the immune system that leads to the destruction of brain cells. Antibodies that attack brain cells have been found in the blood of some people with Alzheimer's disease. (An antibody is a substance produced by the body to combat bacteria, viruses, or other foreign substances.) They have also been found (in lesser concentrations) in the serum of healthy elderly people. It is possible that in Alzheimer's the body responds to its own cells as though they were foreign invaders. Such an autoimmune attack against brain-cell components occurs in multiple sclerosis.

This finding could be explained by a general theory of aging. The theory proposes that as a person ages, certain genes that control the repair of minor damage to chromosomes become less efficient. This may mean that as a person grows older, "errors" creep into his or her genes, leading to the production of defective proteins. The immune system might consider such proteins to be foreign and attack them. If the abnormal proteins are formed in the brain, the result could well be the kind of cell death seen in specific sections of the brains of victims of Alzheimer's disease. Following the destruction of these brain cells, the abnormal proteins might be deposited in tangles outside the brain cells, like trash left in a hallway to be picked up and discarded.

None of these four theories offers a convincing explanation for Alzheimer's disease. It is possible that the disease actually develops from a combination of these factors. Several genes are probably involved, and these in turn must interact with environmental factors (perhaps including viruses) for the disease to develop.

It is also possible that the cause of Alzheimer's disease is entirely different from anything so far suggested. Only continued research and study of the pattern in which the disease affects different groups of people—the epidemiology of the disease—will answer these questions.

• • • •

CHAPTER 5

DIAGNOSIS

Diagnosing Alzheimer's disease is difficult. Psychological depression among victims of the disease confuses the scientist's ability to interpret these people's memory loss and their inability to learn. Other types of dementia must be ruled out before the diagnosis of Alzheimer's can be made. As a document from the National Institutes of Health states, "The doctor must in effect back into a differential diagnosis by discounting first all the other illnesses that might cause senile symptoms."

A doctor must take extraordinary care not to pronounce the diagnosis of Alzheimer's disease hastily because it carries such a dismal prognosis. On the other hand, it is important for a family to know if their relative truly has Alzheimer's disease because in such a case the family will have to make legal, financial, and health-care preparations for the relative. In addition, they may need to know how to interpret memory lapses, bad automobile driving, errors in keeping a checkbook, and strange behavior exhibited by the relative.

Because it is not easy to diagnose Alzheimer's disease, there have been many instances of its incorrect diagnosis in the past. In the mid-1980s, Dr. Leonard L. Heston of the University of Minnesota estimated that as many as 30% of cases of Alzheimer's disease may have been wrongly diagnosed. These people have either been told that they have the disease when they do not, or their cognitive impairment has been incorrectly attributed to a cause other than Alzheimer's disease. At the present time, because of the great awareness of Alzheimer's disease among doctors and the public, it may be that the disease is overdiagnosed.

Making Progress

The good news is that in recent years, the ability to diagnose Alzheimer's disease with simple tests has improved greatly. Purely clinical examinations performed in a physician's office give an accurate diagnosis in about 80% of cases; adding laboratory testing raises this accuracy to 90%. Many of the diagnostic errors recorded in previous years resulted from the failure to recognize depression as a cause of apparent memory loss. Awareness of this complication has greatly increased the diagnostic accuracy for Alzheimer's disease.

In the summer of 1987, a government-sponsored conference concluded that there was "no substitute for a physician's time, expertise, and clinical judgment" in making a correct diagnosis of Alzheimer's disease. It is also important to remember that the ultimate criterion for diagnosing the disease is the progressive appearance and worsening of symptoms, which can only be seen with time.

Two real-life cases, presented below, illustrate the challenge in unraveling the cause of cognitive changes in an elderly person who may have Alzheimer's disease:

Mrs. R. was 85 years old when she was brought to the doctor because she was acting confused. During the examination, the doctor found a lump in Mrs. R.'s breast. This turned out to be a cancer. A brain scan found that her brain had decreased in size, but no more than would be expected at her age. The doctor diagnosed mild dementia, possibly as the result of a recent urinary tract infection Mrs. R. had had and a change in the location where she lived. Mrs. R. had breast surgery and radiation therapy for the cancer.

Following treatment, Mrs. R. had memory problems and difficulty walking. Her walking problem gradually lessened, but her confusion and memory loss continued, although it did not get any worse. She was taking several medications. She was hospitalized again for mental impairment. In the hospital the doctors saw a neatly dressed woman, usually absorbed in reading a magazine or novel. When they asked her what she was reading, Mrs. R. could not name it but showed it to them instead. She was receptive and alert but had a confused stare and an abnor-

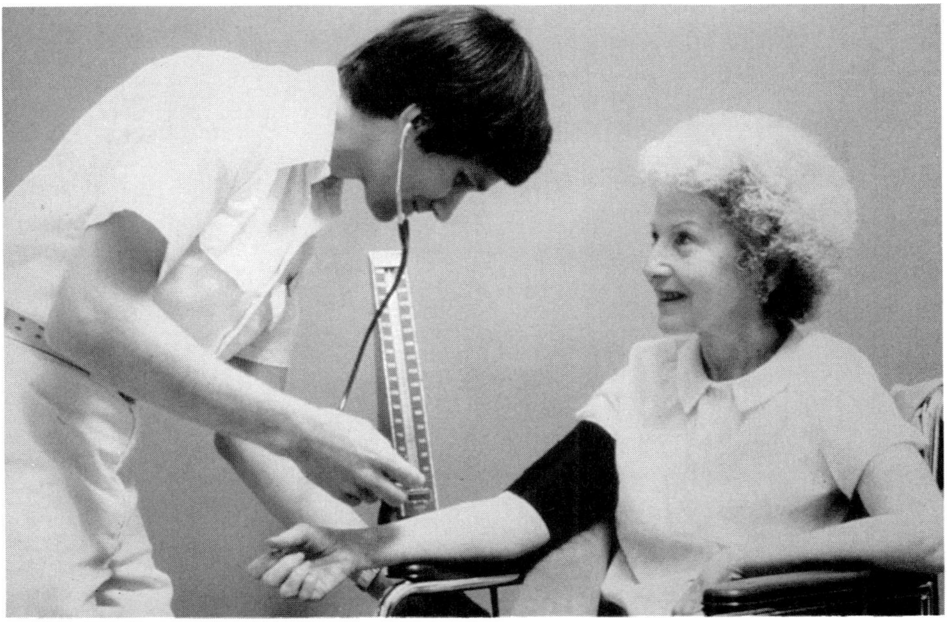

Testing a patient's blood pressure. High blood pressure can lead to multi-infarct dementia, a brain disorder that produces accumulative effects that are similar to those of Alzheimer's.

mal sense of time and place. The doctors tried to test her mathematical skills, but she refused to do the tests. She freely admitted a problem with her memory but said it did not bother her. She did not remember her breast surgery. Her behavior showed no signs of depression.

Mrs. R. probably had Alzheimer's disease, but she might also have been showing certain effects of cancer on the nervous system. The doctors would have to watch her while she stayed in the nursing home for many months, to see whether her loss of mental abilities worsened.

Mr. L. is an elderly man who had been living alone until a few years ago. At that time he had been assaulted and had then had a cardiac arrest.

He recuperated and left the nursing home with good mental abilities. Soon after this, however, his family brought him to a nursing home because he had been acting confused.

Mr. L. makes extravagant claims. He says that he was an executive with a major oil corporation and had traveled all over the world, hunted with former president Jimmy Carter, and knew Theodore Roosevelt at the time of World War I. He says he is 120 years old. He also claims to have been a judge, an attorney, and a teacher of law.

In the nursing home he has acquired the nickname "the Rascal." When asked, who is the president today? Mr. L. replies, "I haven't been up long enough to know." Then he adds, "Mr. Roosevelt. I've known him all my life. He used to be a boy just like me."

The physicians must decide whether Mr. L. has delusions or is kidding around with them. If he is demented, is it because of Alzheimer's disease or one of his previous illnesses? After two years of studying him, the doctors decide that he has Alzheimer's disease.

Faced with such confusing cases, a doctor must know all of the possible causes of such a patient's behavior. In general, Alzheimer's disease accounts for about two-thirds of all dementia in elderly persons. The next largest cause of dementias in the elderly, accounting for 16% of all cases, is another irreversible condition, called multi-infarct dementia. This type of dementia is the consequence of brain damage caused by a series of small strokes or injuries to blood vessels in the brain. Such small strokes may go unnoticed and produce cumulative effects quite similar to the symptoms of Alzheimer's disease.

An "infarct" is the mark left behind by a stroke. It consists of a small mass of coagulating blood and dead tissue. Multiple small infarcts in the blood vessels of the brain can lead to progressive mental and physical decline. Usually, the symptoms of such infarcts are preceded by a history of high blood pressure or a previous stroke. One feature of multi-infarct dementia is that it progresses in a stepwise fashion, in contrast to the steady decline in mental function that occurs in Alzheimer's disease. Because the infarct is usually limited to one part of the brain, the symptoms usually are also limited, or "local"; only one side of the body or a specific faculty may be affected, such as language or shape recognition. In contrast, the symptoms of Alzheimer's disease are "global," affecting the entire mind and body. Infarcts can be seen on a CAT (computerized axial tomography) scan—a form of X-ray examination that produces a three-dimensional image of the body using a computer.

Mistaking multi-infarct dementia for Alzheimer's in demented patients is apparently not a major problem. In a 1986 study, 2 doctors reviewed microscope slides of brain tissue from 76 cases of clinically diagnosed Alzheimer's disease and found that only 2 cases (3%) could be classified as multi-infarct dementia rather than Alzheimer's disease.

Aside from Alzheimer's disease and multi-infarct dementia, the remaining 18% of dementias in elderly persons are due to conditions that are at least partly treatable. It can take considerable skill and effort to detect these less common causes of dementia, which are referred to as "pseudodementias," psychological or metabolic diseases that masquerade as dementia. But the consequences of overlooking such a cause and dooming the patient to an inaccurate diagnosis of Alzheimer's disease and all that it entails are so devastating that a thorough search for the true cause of a patient's dementia is mandatory.

Drug Intoxication: Drug intoxication is the most common cause of forgetfulness, confusion, and disorientation in the aged, many of whom take many different prescription drugs. Some of these drugs, such as the beta-blocking agents and digoxin used for treating heart disease; barbiturates; tranquilizers; antidepressants; the diuretics used to rid the body of excess water in patients with high blood pressure; and antiarthritic drugs can cause confusion and disorientation. These unpleasant side effects may lin-

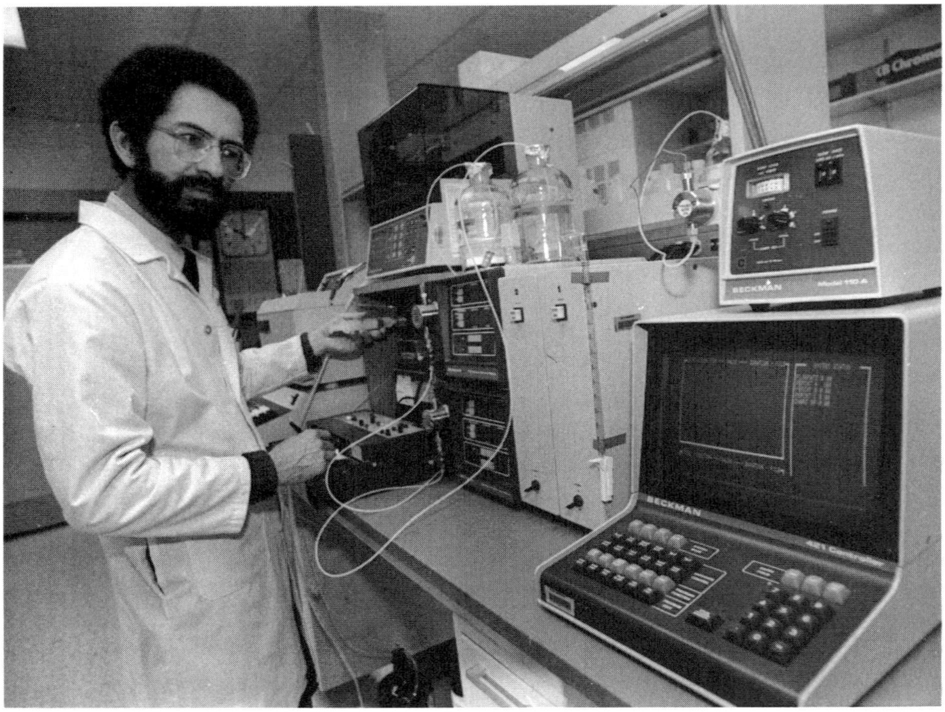

A doctor demonstrates a machine that measures the effects of different vitamins on the aging process. A deficiency of certain vitamins can have adverse effects on the human body and may, in fact, cause dementia.

ger longer in older patients because their liver and kidney functions slow down, and their bodies cannot eliminate drugs as rapidly as younger people do. Many physicians confronted with confused elderly patients simply eliminate all drugs for a trial period. Often, this is sufficient to clear the patient's confusion.

Depression Depression is the second most frequently found cause of apparent dementia in elderly persons. Such symptoms as loss of self-esteem, loneliness, anxiety, and boredom can become more common as elderly persons face retirement, the deaths of relatives and friends, and other such crises—often several at the same time.

What seems to be a depression may also be a realistic emotional reaction to the difficult circumstances that often accompany aging; the loss of income and influence, for example. Such a mood might benefit from sensitive human contact and rewarding activity but should not be considered as either a mental or a physical illness. Depression, however, can also be a consequence of Alzheimer's disease as a person realizes that his or her abilities to remember and to function are fading.

warding activity but should not be considered as either a mental or a physical illness. Depression, however, can also be a consequence of Alzheimer's disease, as a person realizes that his or her abilities to remember and to function are fading.

There are ways to differentiate a true primary depression from depression secondary to, or resulting from, Alzheimer's disease. Depressed people often have had earlier bouts of depression along with symptoms of insomnia, fatigue, or loss of appetite. In contrast, a person in the early stages of Alzheimer's disease often singles out a particular memory problem or a difficulty in doing arithmetic as the reason for his or her depression. The onset of a progressive dementia such as Alzheimer's disease is also likely to be slow and insidious, whereas true depressions usually develop more quickly. If there is a reasonable suspicion that a person's cognitive problems stem from depression, a trial treatment period with antidepressant medication and brief psychotherapy may be appropriate.

Other Causes of Apparent Dementia Some other common metabolic disorders and infections that do not cause mental symptoms in younger people can bring on a dementialike state in older persons. Heart problems, vitamin deficiency, thyroid dysfunction, and sometimes even a bad case of influenza or gastroenteritis can all cause confusion, memory loss, and disorientation in persons above the age of 65. For men and women whose brains have already undergone the normal changes of aging, mental functioning often is maintained only through a delicate balance of compensatory mechanisms, which can easily be affected by stress. A few of the more notable disorders that can lead to symptoms of dementia are as follows:

- Pernicious anemia, a blood disorder caused by an impaired ability to use one of the B vitamins. In older people the first symptoms of pernicious anemia may be irritability or depression.
- Inadequate production of thyroid hormone, which can result in apathy, depression, or dementia.
- Hypoglycemia, a condition in which there is not enough sugar in the blood. This can give rise to confusion or changes in personality. Too little or too much sodium or calcium can also trigger disturbing changes in mental functioning.

- Oxygen shortage caused by heart and lung problems, which are fairly common in elderly persons. A lack of oxygen can starve brain cells and lead to the symptoms of dementia.
- Acquired immune deficiency syndrome (AIDS), which often causes symptoms of dementia. Fortunately, there are very few elderly people with AIDS. The most common way in which older people contract this disease is from blood transfusions, and thanks to the introduction of the AIDS screening test for donated blood, such cases will become even rarer in the future.
- Dementialike symptoms can also be caused by a brain tumor, lead or mercury poisoning, meningitis (infection of the brain), swelling of the brain as a result of injury, pesticides, infection of the brain by the organism that causes syphilis (a contagious, often venereal, disease caused by bacteria), and neurological diseases such as Parkinson's disease and Huntington's chorea, which is a disease of the central nervous system, as well as multiple sclerosis, an incurable disease that affects the brain and spinal cord. If dementia occurs suddenly, it is more likely to be due to a cause other than Alzheimer's disease. Appropriate tests can determine whether any of these conditions are present.

In the Doctor's Office

When you bring a relative who has apparent dementia and suspected Alzheimer's disease to the doctor, the patient will be given an extensive examination to differentiate among all of the possible causes of dementia. The first step will be a thorough investigation of the patient for physical causes of the memory loss and behavior change.

The doctor will then determine the patient's cognitive and mental status to see whether true dementia is present and how severe it is. Early in the course of a dementia many patients still look and behave normally and have the ability to talk normally. Moreover, they may be unaware that they have any cognitive deficits, or they may deny the presence of such problems. This means that the physician will have to perform several tests of cognitive ability to evaluate the patient's status.

A relatively simple way of estimating the severity of a patient's dementia is the mental-status questionnaire examination (MSQ). It consists of 10 simple questions that are good indicators of a person's alertness, orientation to time and place, and recent and remote memory (mental competence). The doctor will try to slip these questions into normal conversation with the patient as an ordinary part of the examination:

- Where are we now?
- Where is this place located?
- What is today's date?
- What month is it?
- What year is it?
- How old are you?
- When is your birthday?
- What year were you born?
- Who is the president of the United States?
- Who was the president before him?

In addition to whether the answers are correct, the doctor observes the patient's manner for hostility, evasiveness, or meaningless talking (confabulation). A score of 9–10 correct answers indicates no confusion; 6–8 correct, slightly confused; 3–5, moderately confused; 0–2, severely confused.

To pick up more subtle degrees of dementia, the doctor will use other tests. For instance, he or she may give the patient a list of three items, such as "brown shoes, red house, Empire State Building." After saying these words to the patient a few times, the doctor asks the patient to recite the items five minutes later. The patient may be asked to give change of a dollar, count backward from 100 by sevens (subtract serial sevens), or follow a three-part instruction: Take this piece of paper in your right hand, fold it in half, and put it on the floor. Other standard tests of cognitive ability are to ask the patient to explain cartoons and interpret proverbs. None of these questions is individually conclusive, but all taken together create an impression of the patient's mental functioning.

Accurate diagnosis of the patient's cognitive problem and its probable cause requires the doctor to learn the details of the history of the problem, such as when it began, what significant events preceded it, and whether it has recently gotten worse. In this quest, the physician may have to turn to the accompanying family member(s) for accurate details, because the suspected dementia often disqualifies the patient as a reliable observer and reporter of past events. Therefore, it is essential that the history be taken from a family member, close friend, or other person who is well acquainted with the patient and who can document any decline in the patient's memory and other cognitive functions.

Including a family member in the history-taking procedure can also help to determine the degree of the patient's dementia in other ways. When interviewed by a physician, the person who has Alzheimer's disease frequently turns to his or her spouse or another immediate observer to supply the details of the history. This is another sign of possible significant memory loss.

Here are some questions that the doctor may ask the patient (or the patient's companion) in order to determine the patient's level of functioning. The list is graded from the simplest task to the most difficult. Can the patient do the following:

- Remain continent in bowel and bladder?
- Move unassisted from bed to chair?
- Get about unassisted on foot or by wheelchair?
- Take care independently of his or her hair, teeth, and personal grooming?
- Dress and undress properly with no help?
- Bathe without assistance?
- Shop, cook, and do ordinary housework?
- Use the telephone?
- Travel alone by public transportation?

This is a sampling of the questions and tests that the doctor will use to explore the patient's cognitive status. Many other similar procedures are used for this purpose as well.

After examining the patient, the physician will order some basic laboratory tests. A government panel commissioned by the

National Institutes of Health in 1987 listed eight particularly useful tests. Among them are a urine analysis for possible infection, an electrocardiogram, a complete count of blood cells, a thyroid-function test, and a measurement of minerals (electrolytes) in the blood. The panel concluded that "most of the readily reversible metabolic, endocrine-deficiency, and infectious states will be revealed by these simple investigations."

A chest X-ray or electroencephalogram (brain-wave pattern) might be appropriate in some situations. Lumbar puncture, in which a sample of spinal fluid is taken through a needle, is not considered to be a very helpful test, unless the patient's dementia has developed very rapidly (within a few months' time), which suggests an infectious disease such as tuberculosis or a fungus infection of the brain.

Imaging Studies

After the physical examination, determination of the patient's mental status, taking of the patient's medical history, and the performance of selected laboratory tests, imaging studies may

Tests using positron emission tomography (PET) show that the brain's intake of oxygen and sugar decreases as Alzheimer's progresses.

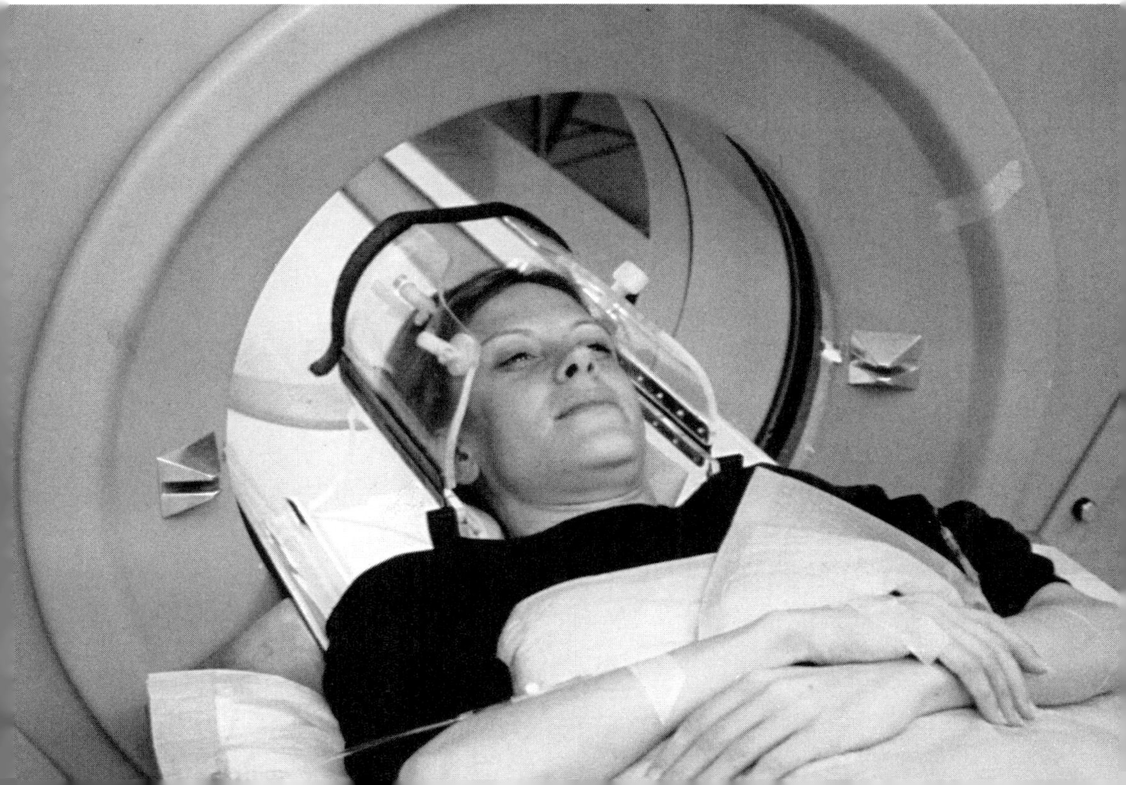

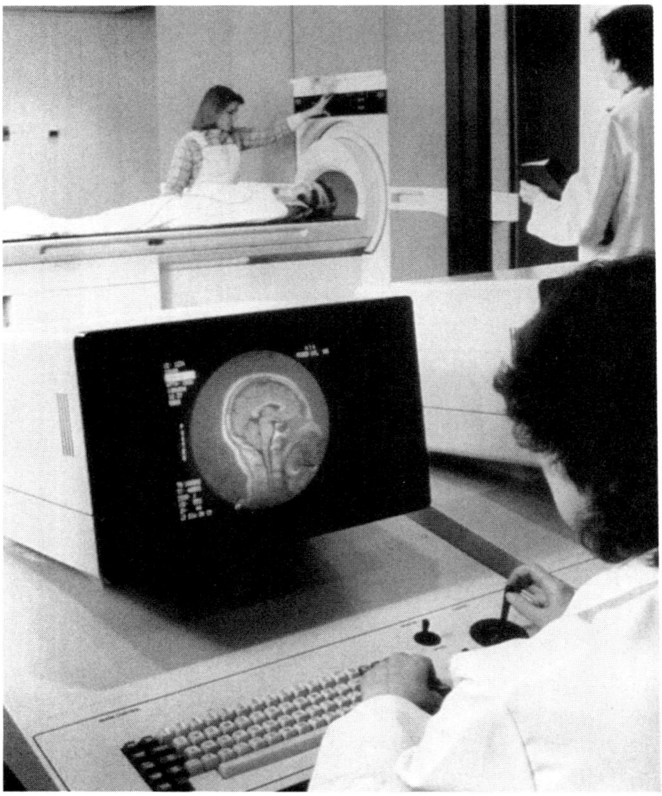

Magnetic resonance imaging (MRI) is more sophisticated than either PET or CAT scans, and can detect extremely subtle alterations in the brain.

help confirm a suspected diagnosis in some cases. But such studies are expensive, and experts agree that the examination and history are usually more informative.

Computer axial tomography (CAT) scanning should be used conservatively, say experts in the field of medical diagnosis. In the case of persons with Alzheimer's disease, CAT scans often show far greater brain shrinkage than that which normally occurs as we grow older. Surprisingly, however, this brain atrophy is not always obvious in Alzheimer's disease, especially in elderly patients. And some people who are still mentally alert may also show a loss of brain tissue. Therefore, CAT scans do not conclusively prove the presence or absence of Alzheimer's disease. However, CAT scans can be useful in evaluating suspected Alzheimer's disease in that they help to exclude other brain disorders, such as multi-infarct dementia, once the existence of dementia has been definitely established in a particular patient.

A newer imaging technique, positron emission tomography (PET), has the potential to become a useful diagnostic tool. It is currently used only for research. Positron emission tomoqraphy measures brain activity rather than brain structure. Scans done by this technique show that as Alzheimer's disease gets worse, there is a substantial decline in the brain's intake of oxygen and the sugar glucose, which are the fuels that brain cells use for their energy needs. Some researchers have shown a correlation between the degree to which glucose use decreases and the degree of cognitive impairment in Alzheimer's disease.

The newest and most expensive imaging procedure, magnetic resonance imaging (MRI), may become more helpful than CAT scans or PET in the future, but for now it, too, is a research tool. The biggest drawback of MRI is its very high cost. MRI employs very high-strength magnetic fields to probe the structure of the soft tissues of the body. It can show alterations in the brain that either are not visible on CAT scans or show up much later.

Whatever an initial thorough examination shows, the ultimate criterion for diagnosing Alzheimer's disease (prior to death and brain autopsy) is a worsening of the symptoms of dementia and physical dysfunction. The doctor's task is to do the basic tests, establish how severe the dementia is, then repeat the tests and examinations for the severity of symptons six months later. If the degree of dementia has not worsened significantly, the patient probably does not have Alzheimer's disease.

A return visit to the doctor's office is scheduled so that he or she can inform the family about the diagnosis and the test results on which it is based. Should the patient be present at this conference? Dr. Albert A. Fisk, medical director of the Wisconsin Geriatric Center in Milwaukee, believes that the patient should be included. Most patients suffering from a mild to moderate case of Alzheimer's disease recognize that they are losing their intellectual abilities. "Withholding information from such a patient serves only to exacerbate the anxiety and depression that often accompany early Alzheimer's disease," Dr. Fisk says. For the family and patient to work together in managing this devastating disease, they need to have an open, trusting relationship. To begin by keeping secrets does not foster trust. (These considerations may not apply to patients with rapid-onset Alzheimer's disease, which is usually already far advanced by the time it is diagnosed.)

At this return visit, the doctor will usually evaluate the course of the patient's loss of cognitive functions. Is it likely to continue? To become better and worse alternately? Might the patient's mental abilities deteriorate rapidly?

The physician, the patient, and the patient's family must also talk about the possibility that the patient will ultimately live in a nursing home. Discussions such as this give both the patient and the patient's family an idea of what the future is likely to hold, so that they can prepare emotionally and medically for various possibilities.

Families of Alzheimer's patients should also be making financial and legal preparations for his or her future (see Chapter 8). The physician should either talk to the family about these necessities or refer the family to a legal counselor who can help them. Referral to any available social-service agencies that provide patient day-care or family-support groups is also helpful.

If the physician judges that the patient is exhibiting symptoms of a depression, he or she can prescribe antidepressant medication. Otherwise, the physician may recommend one of the drugs used to treat dementia, although the family and the patient should be cautioned not to expect that the patient's cognitive skills will dramatically improve when these drugs are used. Drugs currently available for treating dementia, as well as experimental drugs still being evaluated, are described in the next chapter.

• • • •

CHAPTER 6

TREATMENT

FDA headquarters, Washington, D.C.

Although there is not yet a treatment or cure for Alzheimer's disease, research into its chemical basis is proceeding and providing valuable information for testing possible new drugs to be used in its treatment. Such clinical testing may eventually lead to effective drug therapy for Alzheimer's disease. As of this writing, however, no known chemical substance stops or even slows the inevitable loss of mental abilities that occurs in the disease.

However, there are drugs that help control some of the symptoms of Alzheimer's disease and that make it easier for the family to care for its victim at home and for a longer time than was possible in the past. These drugs alleviate the depression that

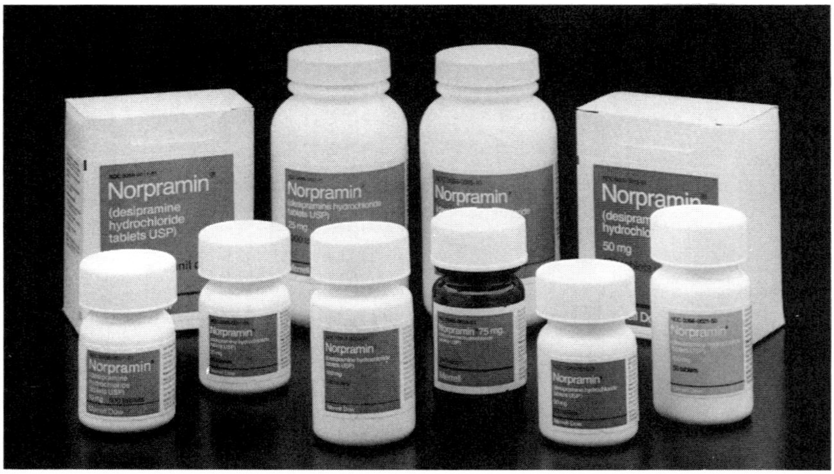

Norpramin and other antidepressant drugs are frequently given to Alzheimer's patients, especially in the early stages of the illness.

often accompanies the patient's realization that his or her mental abilities are fading and also calm the agitated or violent patient. During the course of the illness, nearly every patient receives one or more of these two classes of drugs.

Antidepressants

Antidepressants, such as the tricyclic drugs (this term refers to the drug's chemical structure) imipramine and desipramine, are very commonly given to Alzheimer's patients, especially in the early stages of the illness, when the patient is still aware of his or her loss of memory and thinking ability. According to Dr. Fisk, "Depression accompanying Alzheimer's disease is common, much more common than depression masquerading as dementia." Tricyclic antidepressant drugs should be given in low doses to elderly patients because they are often extremely sensitive to medication.

Antidepressants frequently have unpleasant effects, such as causing difficulty in urinating and producing dizziness when the patient rises from a lying or sitting position. The family should watch the patient carefully for these problems. Urinary retention can lead to infection, and dizziness can lead to falls and injuries. A newer antidepressant drug of a different type, called trazodone, may have less tendency to produce these effects in some patients, although it does cause drowsiness.

Despite their adverse effects, the antidepressant medications seem to help some Alzheimer's disease patients. The behavior of these people often improves, and sometimes it even seems that their mental abilities become sharper for a time.

Unfortunately, Dr. Fisk finds, many elderly patients with Alzheimer's disease do not respond to antidepressants. Their families must use behavioral means, such as family and social activities, to keep these patients as alert as possible.

Tranquilizers

Tranquilizers are the other major class of drugs that are frequently prescribed for Alzheimer's disease patients. These drugs include both the minor tranquilizers, such as Valium (diazepam), and the so-called major tranquilizers (neuroleptics), which are also used to treat schizophrenia and other psychiatric illnesses.

Minor tranquilizers can reduce the nocturnal wandering that some Alzheimer's disease patients engage in. If these milder drugs fail, more powerful antipsychotic neuroleptic drugs, such as Thorazine (chlorpromazine), Haldol (haloperidol), and Navane (thiothixene), can treat this problem. These stronger agents may also be useful if the patient has terrors and hallucinations. They can also be used for the so-called sundown syndrome, in which the patient experiences confusion and agitation at night.

Like antidepressants, however, neuroleptic drugs also have undesirable effects. They can interfere with the patient's movements, causing symptoms similar to Parkinson's disease. Again, the family should watch for these signs, which can occur even with low doses of these drugs in elderly persons.

There has been no clear-cut success in using drugs to treat the primary symptoms of Alzheimer's disease—forgetfulness, loss of the ability to think and calculate, absence of judgment, and difficulty in speaking intelligently. Many drugs have been tried for this purpose, and some have seemed promising for a time, but none are currently considered effective.

Ergoloid Mesylates

A class of compounds called ergoloid mesylates is the only type of chemical substance approved by the U.S. Food and Drug Administration for the treatment of dementia. Ergoloid mesylates are natural chemicals resembling hormones that were discovered in a fungus called ergot that grows on rye and wheat.

Probably the best-known commercial form of this drug class is a mixture of ergoloid mesylates marketed under the name of Hydergine. This drug mixture is thought to improve the metabolism of brain cells by both increasing the blood supply to the brain and by directly stimulating the enzymes in these cells.

Hydergine has been evaluated extensively in patients with Alzheimer's disease. At best, the results can be described as mixed. Some doctors say that the drug increases these patients' energy and mood in a subtle way, but very few investigators claim that it improves their alertness, memory, or overall behavior. Certainly Hydergine does not prevent the deterioration of memory that is typical of the disease.

Drugs to Increase the Concentration of Acetylcholine

When scientists found that a central deficit in the brains of Alzheimer's patients was a lack of enzyme choline acetyltransferase or CAT (see Chapter 3), they determined to administer drug therapy of several kinds to victims of the illness. This discovery also provided researchers a rational basis on which to base tests of new drugs or develop others specifically designed for aspects of the illness. Several approaches have been used in attempts to increase the amount of acetylcholine in the brain of Alzheimer's patients. The dilemma may be like Parkinson's disease, in which a treatment is available even though the cause of cell death in the brain is not known.

Physostigmine was one of the first drugs to be tested for its capacity to increase the concentration of acetylcholine in the brains of patients with Alzheimer's disease. It achieves this effect by knocking out an enzyme that reduces the formation of acetylcholine. There were early reports that the memory of patients treated with physostigmine did improve. In one trial, patients treated with this drug showed an 11% overall improvement in their scores on a memory recognition test. According to Dr. Kenneth L. Davis of New York's Mount Sinai School of Medicine, the scientist who conducted this test, "The [most-improved patients] were made to look like they had [been] 1 1/2 years earlier."

However, this early success with physostigmine, reported in 1984, was not always repeated in later studies. In addition, Dr. Katzman has written that, "Not all investigators have been impressed by the degree of improvement produced by physostigmine." Some of these researchers questioned whether the minor improvement that the drug produced would have any meaningful impact on a patient's life. Nonetheless, the evidence suggested that this approach could lead to something that would help the memory of patients with Alzheimer's disease.

More recently, THA (tetrahydroaminoacridine), a chemical whose action is similar to that of physostigmine, has been in the news. In 1986 Dr. William K. Summers, a psychiatrist in Arcadia, California, reported that THA had produced "dramatic objective improvements" in the mental functioning of 10 of 17 Alzheimer's disease patients in whom it had been tested. According to one news report, Dr. Summers said that patients who did not recogize their children or remember their own names were able to recognize their families again after taking THA.

But many doctors who treat patients with Alzheimer's disease questioned Dr. Summers' report. They believed that Dr. Summers had not used appropriate tests to determine whether his patients had actually improved. A major trial of THA, sponsored by the National Institutes of Health, was quickly set up, but by late 1987 it had been put on hold. About 20% of the first 50 patients who were enrolled in the study showed signs of severe liver damage when they were given THA. The trial ended in the fall of 1987 (it was resumed in the spring of 1988, but lower doses of the drug were tested). Although many doctors have confirmed that this side effect of THA is not irreversible, in 1988 the U.S. Food and Drug Administration prohibited the use of THA as a treatment for Alzheimer's disease.

Increasing the dietary intake of choline and lecithin, two substances that the body can use to manufacture acetylcholine, has also been tested in Alzheimer's disease and other dementias. But this approach has had no reproducible or verifiable benefit, and people who buy these supplements at health-food stores are probably not accomplishing anything by using them, although they are probably not risking much harm, either.

Scientists think that an ideal drug for persons with Alzheimer's disease may be an acetylcholine agonist, a drug that perfectly mimics acetylcholine in its effects but does not have to be processed by the CAT enzyme in order to become active in the brain and nervous system. Unfortunately, currently known chemicals of this type are either too short-lived in the body or have bad side effects.

In 1984, doctors at the Dartmouth Medical School in Hanover, New Hampshire, pumped bethanechol, a compound that is an acetylcholine agonist, directly into the brain fluid of four patients with Alzheimer's disease. The physicians reported very favorable results. But in this instance, too, it turned out that the doctors had used unreliable tests to gauge the drug's effect. Further research into the effects of bethanechol therapy in a small number of patients is still in progress.

A number of other substances have been administered to Alzheimer's patients in tests without lasting benefit. They include the following:

- Piracetam is a compound thought to stimulate the overall generalized electrical activity of the brain. There is no conclusive evidence that piracetam by itself is effective in slowing the deterioration of intellectual functioning that characterizes Alzheimer's disease.
- Chelating agents remove aluminum that may collect in the brain in Alzheimer's disease and can damage nerve cells. In two trials conducted in 1983, none of the patients who were treated with chelating agents got significantly better.

A hyperbaric chamber, which creates conditions of heightened air pressure and a pure oxygen environment, has been used as a treatment for Alzheimer's disease but has not produced significant results.

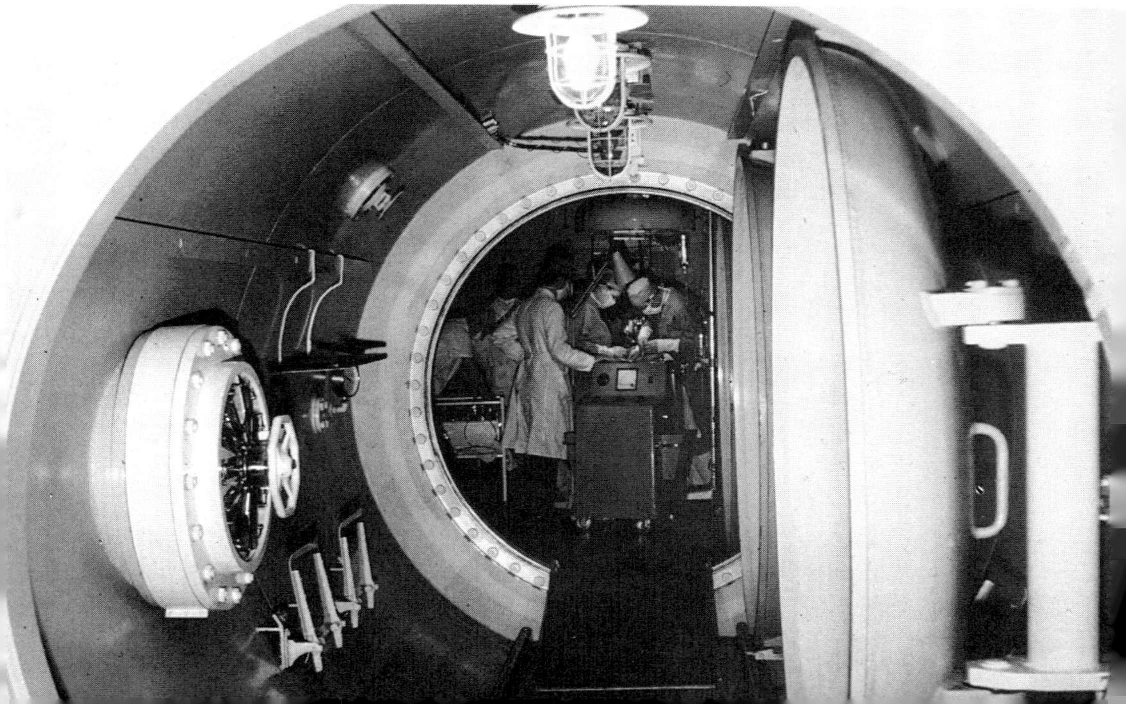

- Vasopressin, a hormone formed by the pituitary gland, and which has sometimes been found to increase learning in rats, has also been tested in patients with Alzheimer's disease. So far, no research group has announced favorable results with this substance.
- In 1983, naloxone, a compound used to block the action of heroin, was reported to be beneficial for improving memory retention in Alzheimer's patients. However, scientists who performed later studies were unable to confirm this report.
- The use of high-potency vitamin preparations has been advocated with enthusiasm from time to time, but there is little evidence that they produce any benefit in patients who do not have specific vitamin deficiencies.
- Extracts of blue-green algae have occasionally been promoted to treat Alzheimer's disease, but there is no evidence for their efficacy, and they may well be harmful. Consumers should be particularly cautious about using these compounds because they are officially classed as "food additives," rather than as drugs, and therefore are not subject to government reviews of their safety.
- Hyperbaric oxygen therapy, which involves enclosing a patient in a chamber containing oxygen under very high pressure, has also been tried in Alzheimer's disease but has produced no clear improvement.
- A naturally occurring hormone, nerve growth factor, when injected into the brains of animal subjects, has increased the activity of the enzyme choline acetyltransferase (CAT). Its use is based on the idea that nerve cells require hormones for health and growth, just as other tissues in the body do, and that nerve growth factor may be one such hormone. It has not yet been tested in humans.
- Brain transplants represent another way in which Alzheimer's disease may resemble Parkinson's disease. Surgeons have experimentally transplanted parts of the adrenal gland and sections of fetal brain tissue into the brains of Parkinson's patients in order to restore messenger substances that were lost as a result of cell death in various regions of the patients' brains. Perhaps similar experiments will be tried in patients with Alzheimer's disease, although such an attempt is not likely in the near future.

Scientists are constantly testing possible treatments for Alzheimer's disease. Many of these treatments appear to provide substantial benefit the first time they are tried. Unfortunately, subsequent trials typically fail to reproduce the initial success, which may be the result of factors other than the actual treatment—such as physical or mental stimulation merely from being included in an experiment or the desire to please the doctors or scientists performing a medical study. A booklet published by the National Institute of Neurological and Communicative Diseases and Stroke accurately expresses the need for caution in evaluating new and experimental treatments for Alzheimer's disease: "Repeated trials of any drug under controlled conditions, and long-term follow-up of patients are always necessary before judgments can be made," says the booklet, and it points out that "this is where many drug 'bonanzas' fail the test."

• • • •

CHAPTER 7

CARING FOR PATIENTS AND FAMILIES

Caring for a patient with Alzheimer's disease is a difficult, often thankless task. One medical student studying Alzheimer's patients in a nursing home said, "We may be on the brink of sensational discoveries down the road, but right now it's just hard work." The British doctor Sir Martin Roth, commenting on the death of Alzheimer's patients, observed, "It looks like death from boredom."

The bulk of the burden of caring for Alzheimer's victims falls on their families as home care is usually the option selected. But just because the doctor has no restorative drugs to prescribe and the patient is not in the hospital does not mean that the doctor has no role to play in the patient's care. On the contrary, the families of Alzheimer's disease patients can expect their physicians to act as counselors who can help them maintain the patient's quality of life and keep the patient active as long as possible.

Keeping the patient alert and active is accomplished, in part, by a conscious effort to help the patient remain oriented in regard to time and place. One way to do this is to provide constant and continuous cues to stimulate the patient. These cues may include prominently color-coded calendars, clocks, and checklists to facilitate orientation; access to night-lights, radio, and television to minimize sensory deprivation; and the placement of photographs and other objects around the house to help create a familiar, and therefore stable, environment.

However, activity requires energy. Therefore, the patient should get adequate rest, because fatigue may exacerbate disorientation and irritability. Another consideration is to maintain the patient's

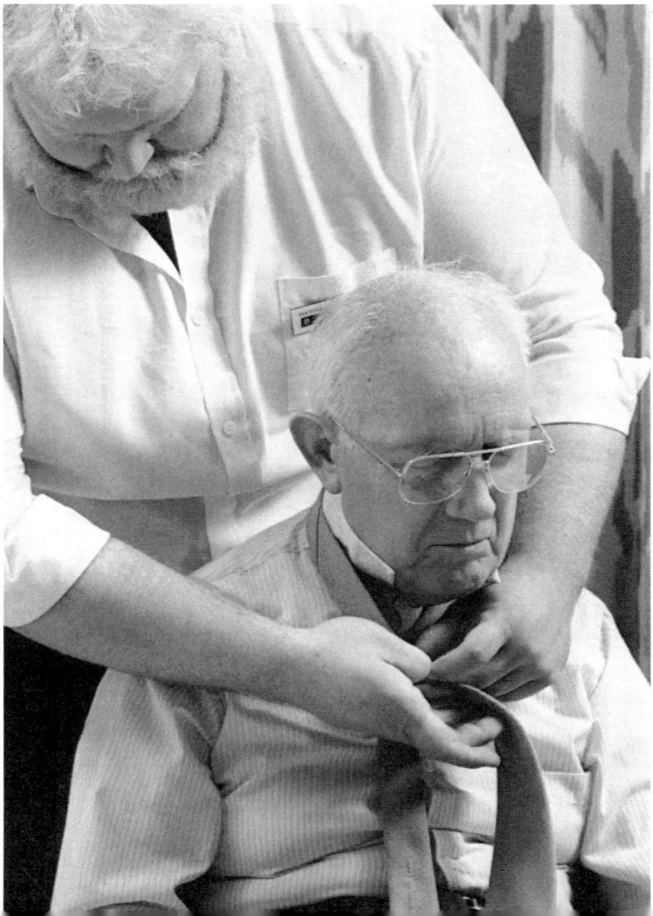

Nursing home facilities should be able to tend to the physical and emotional needs of their patients by providing round-the-clock medical care and by keeping the patient as physically active as possible.

mobility, which means designing the patient's environment in such a way as to prevent falls and other accidents.

The patient should also be encouraged to interact with others for as long as possible. This can be difficult when a person cannot read, converse, or even follow the plot of a television show. The family needs to find out what their relative with Alzheimer's disease can still do and encourage him or her to do it. As a document produced by the National Institutes of Health points out, "Long after he has been forced to stop working on his car, a person with Alzheimer's disease may still be able to sing along to old tunes on the radio."

Patients in the later stages of Alzheimer's disease can be especially difficult to care for. Taking care of an adult who behaves in large measure like an infant is a taxing chore. At this point, one wife of an Alzheimer's disease patient said her task was like "chasing a six-foot toddler around the house."

Stretching the Family's Resources

The government report entitled *Losing a Million Minds* revealed interesting facts about the persons who care for Alzheimer's disease patients. The bulk of informal care is delivered first by spouses, then by children (especially daughters). The burden falls disproportionately on women. The very late onset of most dementing illnesses often means that a woman in her fifties or even late sixties may be the primary care giver.

The burden on all care givers can be great. One survey cited in *Losing a Million Minds* found that 28% of persons taking care of dependent mothers had quit their jobs to give care at home, and a similar proportion had reduced their working hours and were considering leaving their jobs.

Facts like these led gerontologist Robert Binstock, M.D., of Cleveland's Case Western Reserve University, to observe in 1986 that "family abandonment of older persons is a myth. Indeed, families are probably already stretched to their limits in providing physical, emotional, social and financial support for their chronically ill and disabled older relatives."

A survey conducted at Johns Hopkins University and published in the *Journal of the American Medical Association* (*JAMA*) in 1982 stated that the biggest problems people had caring for Alzheimer's disease patients involved "catastrophic reactions"—extreme emotional reactions by the patient, precipitated by the inability to accomplish a task. The patient may exhibit an outburst of anger, lash out physically in response to a request to do something, argue, resist care, or burst out crying from stress or frustration.

Night wandering, which can be frightening for both the patient and his or her family, is another common problem. Care givers to Alzheimer's patients can lose hours of sleep trying to locate their loved ones, who may be lost or injured. Because of this, it is especially important to have many options for coping with—and trying to prevent—night wandering. Some tactics that family members have found successful include the following:

- Restricting napping by the patient during the day; gradually reducing the family's activity before bedtime.
- Taking the patient for an evening walk.
- Providing a secure place for the patient to wander in.
- Keeping all doors to the outside securely locked.
- Having the patient wear an identification bracelet with the words *memory-impaired* engraved on it, in addition to his or her name, address, and phone number.
- Removing doorknobs and placing locks at the bottom of doors near the floor.
- Trying to hide doors by placing things in front of them.
- Making sure photographs of the patient are available to aid in a search in case the patient does get out.

Police are frequently called on to handle the last problem, but often they cannot tell an Alzheimer's disease patient from a vagrant. In western New York State, an Alzheimer's Disease and Related Disorders Association chapter set up the Wandering Adult Program in cooperation with the Erie County sheriff's department. The purpose is to help police "to feel out the situation and not treat dementia victims like alcoholics or vagrants." Demented patients may strike out in fear and paranoia at police, provoking a potentially harmful reaction. In the Wandering Adult Program, police are taught to understand and deal with these and other behavioral reactions.

According to the survey published in the JAMA about problems in caring for Alzheimer's disease patients, suspicion and accusatory behavior affect up to two-thirds of these patients and their families. This particular problem often represents an effort by the brain-injured person to explain misplaced possessions or misinterpreted events. Keeping a very orderly house and putting up signs that point to where objects are kept may help the patient locate things and therefore diminish the frustration that leads to such behavior.

Finally, the JAMA survey discussed the most common safety problems experienced by Alzheimer's disease patients, stressing that they were caused by three common activities—driving, smoking, and cooking. All of these activities are an ordinary part of life, and persons with Alzheimer's disease may be reluctant to give them up. The authors of the JAMA article suggested removing stove knobs, locking some rooms, and locking up matches as several means of preventing accidents. Driving represents mobility and independence in our society, where even teenagers often have access to a car, and losing the privilege of driving can have a severe psychological impact. Nevertheless, persons with fairly advanced stages of Alzheimer's disease are no longer competent to drive. "Patients will often stop driving on orders of their physician," the JAMA survey noted. "If not, the state motor vehicle bureau should be contacted."

Care givers themselves also reported experiencing a number of recurring problems. Very common was feeling angry, sad, depressed, or tired most of the time. Half of the persons caring for Alzheimer's victims felt that they had given up friends, hobbies, or jobs, or felt they had little or no time for themselves. Half also said that they felt that other family members were not doing their share of care giving or were critical of them. Some people had difficulty assuming new roles and responsibilities when they had to do the jobs of both their disabled spouses and themselves. Married people who were taking care of a parent with Alzheimer's disease frequently experienced marital stress.

Several factors can aggravate the problems of care givers. At least in the early stages of Alzheimer's disease, the patient may show some recognition of what the care giver is doing and some gratitude for it. But in the later stages of the disease—when the most personal care is needed—care giving is made more difficult by the inability of the patient to recognize the care giver, acknowledge the help he or she is giving, or show even the slightest appreciation for that help; in fact, the patient may even actually respond angrily at the person offering help.

The Life and Death of Rita Hayworth

In 1976 the press reported that a shaky and disheveled Rita Hayworth had to be helped off a transatlantic flight after it had landed in London. The implication of the story was that the actress had become an alcoholic who could not control her behavior in public. It was not until four years later that doctors discovered that Hayworth's behavior was not due solely to alcohol abuse, but that she was a victim of Alzheimer's disease.

One of the most popular movie personalities of the 1940s, Rita Hayworth was born Margarita Cansino in 1918 and began her career as a dancer. In 1937, Hayworth signed a seven-year contract with Columbia Studios and subsequently made films with Gene Kelly, Fred Astaire, and a host of other leading men. During World War II, Hayworth's stunning beauty as well as her dancing and acting talent led to a series of pinup poses and a definite place among Hollywood's top stars.

Rita Hayworth in the 1946 film Gilda.

Hayworth's private life was also celebrated, if rather tumultuous; among her five husbands were the film director Orson Welles and the Islamic prince Aly Khan, both of whom fathered daughters by her. After her marriage to Khan, however, Hayworth's career began to falter, and during the 1950s and 1960s she began drinking heavily. During the 1970s she tried to establish a career on Broadway but was unsuccessful because she was unable to remember her lines. It is quite possible that Hayworth's memory lapses were, in fact, early symptoms of Alzheimer's disease.

In 1977 a court assigned an administrator to handle Hayworth's affairs on the basis of a report that stated the actress was "unable or unwilling to accept responsibility for her treatment and is a chronic alcoholic." Four years later, after Alzheimer's disease was diagnosed, she was put in the legal charge of her daughter Princess Yasmin Khan. From 1981 until Hayworth's death in 1987, Princess Yasmin cared for and tended to the needs of her mother. The princess also publicized Hayworth's condition, which in the early 1980s was a mysterious disease that few people had heard of. She became involved in the Alzheimer's Disease and Related Disorders Association (ADRDA), an organization concerned with making the public more aware of the illness through educational programs and extensive research.

Not surprisingly, Princess Yasmin experienced a wide range of difficult feelings during the time that she took care of her mother. "I was constantly feeling different emotions," she recalls. "Anger, helplessness, guilt. I kept asking myself, 'Am I doing enough, is there more I can do, and why can't I do more to relieve her anguish?' " But although Hayworth's ordeal was a painful one for both the actress and her daughter, it has led to widespread research into the causes of—and possible cures for—Alzheimer's disease.

Care givers are often their own worst enemies, holding themselves up to an impossible standard. Relaxing that standard is the best thing a care giver can do for him- or herself. The daughter of an Alzheimer's disease patient wrote in the ADRDA newsletter, "This stress can be lessened only if we allow it to be." Her suggestions included the following:

- Don't try to be superhuman—allow other family members to help. In fact, insist on it.
- Learn to deal with offensive behavior from the patient. Ignore it if you can; or leave the room until you calm down.
- Don't hate yourself if you get angry and yell at the patient. You are only human.
- Make sure you get enough rest. Take whatever precautions are necessary so that the patient does not become endangered during night wandering.
- Accept that the situation is difficult. The patient will not get better no matter what you do. It is reasonable to become upset.
- Stay socially active.

Care givers do need support and help from their families. They may also want to try "respite-care" sources, which provide periodic care for the patient so that the primary care-giver can have a break from this demanding task.

Respite care can be provided by a care giver who comes to the house to take care of the patient for a period of time, or by day-care programs, which offer a social setting structured especially for the Alzheimer's disease patient.

Care in the home may be provided by paid home companions or homemakers, who prepare meals, take care of the patient's personal needs, and act as companions for a few hours, an entire day, overnight, or for a weekend.

But obtaining this type of help is not easy. For one thing, support services are very difficult to find in most areas. Another problem is finding services, because they are scattered among many social service agencies. As a result, many people do not make use of such services even where they are available. According to a government report, this is one of the biggest hurdles faced by the families of patients with Alzheimer's disease.

Another obstacle in terms of outside care can be its cost, which may run from $5 to $20 an hour.

Home-care services are difficult to provide and ideally should be provided by people who are specially trained to handle the specific problems of Alzheimer's disease patients—such as memory impairment and loss of intellectual function.

Day-Care Programs

A final obstacle in caring for persons with Alzheimer's disease is psychological: The families of such persons are often reluctant to accept help from outside sources. In some places where support services are available, they are not fully utilized. Carolyn J. French of the Atlanta chapter of the ADRDA tells of a rezoning hearing that was held in that city to set up a residence for persons with Alzheimer's disease. A woman whose husband was afflicted came to the hearing and argued against the residence. She said that family members should be cared for at home, as she had done for her husband. Because this attitude is common, one of the major tasks of workers at local ADRDA chapter offices is helping families accept help.

Day-care programs for persons with Alzheimer's disease must be carefully organized. According to Ms. French, "In a day-care center you create the illusion that the patient is in a normal environment and that they can do things. But you're doing 70–80% of the work and the communication." The goal of a day-care center is to enhance whatever abilities the patient still has, such as playing the piano or dancing. Workers in day-care progams find that for Alzheimer's disease patients music is the most universally enjoyed activity. It brings back pleasant memories, especially the singing of old songs or hymns. One Alzheimer's disease patient who had been a local baseball star when he was young now loves to play catch with the staff at his day-care center. A major focus at day-care centers is on what Ms. French calls "activities geared for success." These may include gardening or crafts, such as making holiday decorations.

It makes no sense to try to teach the patient new skills. Greater success is found in activities that take advantage of old skills or that offer social interaction, such as sing-alongs and visits from children and pets, and those that allow considerable physical activity. Less useful are quiet games such as bingo and activities that require fine motor and language skills, such as movies or current-events discussions.

Daily activities at day-care centers are best organized according to a strict timetable, even with periods as short as 20-minute blocks of time. This is to provide patients with a structured environment and to keep them from becoming disoriented. Shuffling the order of events each day may be necessary to prevent boredom with cognitively normal persons, but it can confuse the patient with Alzheimer's disease. Meals should be planned for the same time each day and should be used as an opportunity for fostering sociability.

A good day-care center for patients with Alzheimer's disease will have lots of open space so that it is easy to keep track of the patients. It should also have a safe, enclosed outdoor exercise area accessible to the patients. Doors may be fitted with a bell or buzzer that alerts the staff when a patient goes outside. A good center should also occasionally have outings to familiar places, such as a zoo, a shopping center, or a restaurant.

Patients who attend these day-care centers once or twice each week usually respond well to them. According to one care giver, "My mother says that she has enjoyed her day when I ask her each time I pick her up at the center. She can't remember what she did or what she had for lunch, but she does seem to enjoy herself."

The staff of a day-care center for Alzheimer's disease patients should include a few supervisory personnel—at least a social worker and a nurse—and many trained program assistants. There should be approximately one program assistant for every four patients. The staff must be able to work with the patients in a caring way but cannot get caught up in their lives. Ideally, the worker at a day-care center for persons with Alzheimer's disease should be patient, flexible, compassionate, and consistently positive and upbeat.

Several innovative demonstration programs are now exploring new ways to provide respite care for Alzheimer's patients. One such program, conducted by the ADRDA under a quarter-million-dollar grant, is establishing an in-home respite-care system. The project will demonstrate the feasibility of training "senior-companion" volunteers as in-home care providers.

The Robert Wood Johnson Foundation and the ADRDA are funding other projects to demonstrate that comprehensive, cost-effective services can be provided to victims of dementia and their care givers. These projects will provide adult day-care centers and support services for dementia patients and their families.

Nursing-care Facilities

When the patient with Alzheimer's disease becomes truly incapacitated, a move to a nursing-care facility is appropriate. Openings in such homes are difficult to find. The family may also suffer considerable guilt in no longer being able to care for their loved one. A compassionate physician can support the family so that it can accomplish the move with a minimum of guilt.

It is not always easy to know when the transition to a nursing-care facility should occur. Writing in the newsletter of the ADRDA, Juliette Warshauer, the wife of an Alzheimer's disease patient, suggested asking the following questions:

- Does the patient know where he or she is? Would a change in environment make a difference?
- Does the patient know who the care giver is? Does he or she respond to the care giver?
- Is constant care required that is beyond the physical capacity of the care giver?
- Can a safe environment be provided for the patient at all times at home?

Home-care services such as the Visiting Nurses of New York provide care for a wide variety of ailments, ranging from temporary incapacitation to serious degenerative conditions such as Alzheimer's disease.

The nursing home must provide for the patient's emotional and social—as well as physical and medical—needs. It is a good idea to visit several facilities before choosing one. During this process, the family should consider whether the nursing home has adequate safety provisions (i.e., fire alarms, protection against night wandering); whether nurses are available 24 hours a day; whether a physician makes frequent visits; what the dining facilities are like; and most important, how the patients are treated. Are they encouraged to socialize and be active? Are they oversedated to keep them quiet? Is there enough space for physical activity? Not all Alzheimer's disease patients, after all, are physically incapacitated.

Because the behavior of patients with Alzheimer's disease can be disruptive, some nursing homes separate them from the other residents. As long as the staff members are trained in how to manage these patients, supervised activities are provided, and the use of restraints and drugs is de-emphasized, separate care for Alzheimer's disease patients can be a benefit rather than a drawback.

Placing the patient with Alzheimer's disease in a nursing home is extremely difficult for the care giver because it is a sharp reminder that the patient will never get better and is nearing the terminal stages of his or her illness. Ms. Warshauer points out the constant reminders of loss experienced by the spouse of an Alzheimer's disease patient when he or she must finally be moved to a nursing facility. They include everything from buying groceries for only one person to learning all over again how to go to social events, this time as a single person. Worst of all, however, is the pain of losing a loved one who is still alive. As Juliette Warshauer says, "Coping with separation presents very real problems for the spouse, who is neither widowed nor divorced, yet must face feelings of loss, loneliness, and guilt which accompany the decision-making process and the actual experience of nursing-home placement."

• • • •

CHAPTER 8

FINANCIAL AND LEGAL ISSUES

Are persons who develop Alzheimer's disease immediately declared legally incompetent? Do they automatically lose the right to handle their own financial and legal affairs? The answer to both of these questions is no. There are, however, legal complications that often arise after a diagnosis of Alzheimer's disease is made. The patient and various members of the patient's family may come into contention with one another over disposal of the patient's property.

Fortunately, there are steps one can take to minimize this kind of problem.

First, every person—whether or not he or she is a victim of Alzheimer's disease—should have a will. It should be prepared carefully, with a lawyer present, so that it will hold up if contested. A will is a document that specifies the way in which a person wants his or her property and estate to be disposed after that person dies. It is possible for a person to change his or her will after he or she is found to have Alzheimer's disease, but it is important that a lawyer be present and also that some sort of proof—such as a witness or videocassette recording—be used to prove that the person was of sound mind, or in a "lucid interval," at the time the will was rewritten.

Another document that every healthy person—as well as persons with Alzheimer's disease—should think about drafting is a living will, which leaves instructions about what should be done in the event that the person becomes so sick as only to be kept alive by artificial means. It is important to note that laws concerning both wills and living wills vary from one state to another.

Once someone is diagnosed as having Alzheimer's disease, that person should see a lawyer to discuss the legal options he or she has. One possibility is for the person to give a relative or someone else the durable power of attorney, meaning that the person so designated is empowered to handle the patient's financial affairs, such as those involving the patient's property and estate. Ob-

This residence was established specifically for the care of elderly childless women. Nursing-home care for Alzheimer's patients is terribly expensive; caregivers can go bankrupt paying for these services.

viously the person chosen to do this—who is called the attorney-in-fact—should be someone the patient trusts; most often, a durable power of attorney is granted to a close family member.

Another thing the patient may want to do is to designate a medical proxy, a person who is entrusted to make medical decisions for the patient—such as when to place the patient in a nursing home. Again, laws concerning this vary from state to state. In some states, the attorney-in-fact has the right to make medical as well as financial decisions for the patient.

The person who is selected as the attorney-in-fact assumes responsibility for the patient immediately, rather than after the patient is declared legally incompetent. Persons with Alzheimer's disease who wish to remain in control of their affairs for a longer time may opt for a springing power of attorney, in which the attorney-in-fact comes into effect only when the patient becomes incompetent. The problem here is that even before incompetency is declared, the patient will go through a period in which he or she is sometimes lucid and sometimes mentally incompetent. This can make it extremely difficult to decide whether the patient is competent enough to make his or her own decisions on a given day. Opting for a durable power of attorney may therefore be a simpler, if more immediately drastic, solution.

The only way in which any person can be declared incompetent is through a specific legal proceeding. Someone—usually a member of the person's family—submits to the court a petition requesting that the person be declared incompetent. If the judge grants the request, the court will then appoint a conservator to handle the person's affairs. If the person has already given someone a durable power of attorney, the court will often assign the attorney-in-fact to be the conservator of the person's property. In some states the person can choose in advance whom he or she wants the conservator to be. If no provisions have been made in advance, the court will usually choose a close family member to act as the person's conservator.

The Financial Ordeal

Another agonizing aspect of Alzheimer's disease is the financial burden it imposes. Nursing homes are devastatingly expensive. The patient's spouse or family can literally go bankrupt paying for these services.

Why is this? Very simply, because by and large neither private insurance plans nor government-sponsored insurance programs cover the long-term nursing-home care that patients with Alzheimer's disease require. The consequence of this omission was described by gerontologist Stanley Brody of the University of Pennsylvania in November 1986. Brody said that 1 of every 20 elderly Americans, and often their families as well, faces financial ruin because of the inability to pay the enormous costs of vitally needed long-term health care. Many people in their forties, fifties, and sixties face the problem of paying $20,000 to $35,000 a year to have a parent cared for in a satisfactory nursing home; of putting the parent in a substandard nursing home; or of absorbing the emotional and economic costs of maintaining the parent in their own home. A large proportion of these people are the children of Alzheimer's disease victims.

According to *Losing a Million Minds,* a large proportion of the cost of nursing-home care for victims of the disease is paid for by individuals. This amounted to $16 billion in 1986.

Much of this cost is borne by the spouses of patients with Alzheimer's disease, who are themselves elderly and often living on a pension. The result is that many of these people literally go bankrupt. After 13 months of nursing home care, 70% of elderly people (including the spouses of persons receiving this care) are below the poverty line.

Government insurance is not designed to cover these problems. Medicare, which is a government-sponsored insurance program for the aged, is not a long-term care plan; it covers less than 2% of expenditures for nursing-home care. Medicaid, another insurance plan set up by the government, is a program intended for the indigent, and eligibility for this program is contingent upon nearly complete depletion of one's financial resources.

Private insurance plans with coverage for long-term care facilities are becoming more available. But they have a major drawback—they do not cover Alzheimer's disease. This is because the disease requires so much nursing-home care that it would be disastrous for a private insurance company to cover it.

The U.S. Congress is working on a "spousal impoverishment" provision in its health-care spending bills. Lawmakers in both the Senate and the House of Representatives have called for a change in the way in which family income and assets are counted

A social worker with an Alzheimer's victim at an adult day health center in Massachusetts. Competent and compassionate attention to the emotional needs of such patients can help ease their fear and suffering.

for the purpose of determining Medicaid eligibility. The spousal impoverishment provision has not yet been passed by Congress, but would provide a moderate amount of help for families of Alzheimer's disease patients if it were to be enacted into law.

It seems unfair that the family of someone with Alzheimer's disease should have to face such financial hardships in addition to all of the other problems posed by this cruel disease. First they see a loved one, usually a parent or spouse, decline in mental ability. Then they are told that their loved one faces a long, untreatable illness and will slowly lose the intellectual powers that make him or her distinctly human. The family witnesses the patient deteriorating day by day before their eyes. Finally, when their relative becomes so incompetent that he or she cannot be cared for at home, the family has to confront the formidable tasks of finding a nursing home for the relative and paying the cost of that care.

Reason to Hope

Under these circumstances, it is amazing that people who care for a relative with Alzheimer's disease do as well as they do. But, in fact, spouses and children do care for their loved ones who are stricken with the disease. Day by day, they do get through the difficulties it poses. And some individuals and families even grow stronger through their pain.

The task of those who care for persons with Alzheimer's disease has improved in many ways during the 1980s. Discussion of the disease has come out into the open so that the relatives of its victims at least no longer need feel alone or anonymous. Support groups have formed rapidly since the organization of ADRDA in 1980. Day care and respite care, although not nearly available enough, are being recognized as necessities for patients with Alzheimer's disease and are becoming much more easy to obtain. And Congress is beginning to address the financial problems faced by the families of patients with the disease.

In the longer run we can hope that the causes of Alzheimer's disease will be understood and that treatments, preventive measures, and perhaps even cures for this illness will be found. There is every reason to hope for significant progress toward these achievements by the time the present generation of young people reaches the vulnerable age for Alzheimer's disease. Research on the illness has increased vigorously since 1983, and several major discoveries about the disease have already been made. Drug trials have been organized and, although the substances so far tested have not proved effective, medical scientists have ideas for new and more ingenious therapies.

In the toll it takes on the human spirit, Alzheimer's disease is truly a modern scourge. Yet as all profound challenges do, confronting this illness evokes the best in the human spirit, in the relatives, nurses, and doctors who care for patients with Alzheimer's disease, and in the scientists who devote their efforts to conquering this enemy of humanity.

• • • •

APPENDIX: FOR MORE INFORMATION

The following is a list of organizations able to provide additional information and/or assistance.

Alzheimer's Disease and Related
Disorders Association, Inc.
70 East Lake Street
Suite 600
Chicago, IL 60601
(800) 621-0379
(800) 572-6037 (in Illinois)

Burke Rehabilitation Center
Community Relations
785 Mamaroneck Avenue
White Plains, NY 10605
(914) 948-0050
(It is necessary to request information specifically on Alzheimer's disease.)

Children of Ageing Parents
2761 Trenton Road
Levittown, PA 19056
(215) 547-1070

Geriatric Study and Treatment Program
Department of Psychiatry
New York University Medical Center
Millhauser Laboratories
550 First Avenue
New York, NY 10016
(212) 340-5700

National Geriatrics Society (NGS)
212 West Wisconsin Avenue,
3rd floor
Milwaukee, WI 53203
(414) 272-4130

National Institute on Aging
Information Center
2209 Distribution Circle
Silver Spring, MD 20910
(This agency provides free pamphlets on Alzheimer's disease and other forms of dementia.)

National Institute on Aging
Information Office
9000 Rockville Pike
Building 31, Room 5C35
National Institutes of Health
Bethesda, MD 20892
(301) 496-1752

National Institute of Neurological and Communicative Disorders and Stroke
Office of Scientific and Health Reports
Building 31, Room 8A06
National Institutes of Health
Bethesda, MD 20892
(301) 496-5751

FURTHER READING

Alzheimer's Disease and Related Disorders Association. *Understanding Alzheimer's Disease.* New York: Scribners, 1988.

Barnes, Deborah M. "Defect in Alzheimer's Is on Chromosome 21." *Science* 235 (February 20, 1987): 846–847.

Bruun, Ruth Dowling, M.D., and Bertel Bruun, M.D. *The Human Body: Your Body and How It Works.* New York: Random House, 1982.

Clark, Matt, et al. "A Slow Death of the Mind." *Newsweek* 106 (December 3, 1984): 56–62.

Cohen, Donna, and Carl Eisdorfer. *The Loss of Self.* New York: Norton, 1986.

Collins, Glenn. "Providing a Respite for Alzheimer's Families." *New York Times,* June 2, 1986, 19.

Danforth, Art. *Living With Alzheimer's Disease: Ruth's Story.* Falls Church, VA: Prestige Press, 1986.

Donner, Carol. *The Magic Anatomy Book.* New York: Freeman, 1986.

Edwards, Diane D. "A Common Medical Denominator." *Science News* 129 (January 25, 1986): 60–62.

Frank, Julia. *Alzheimer's Disease: The Silent Epidemic.* Minneapolis, MN: Lerner Publications, 1985.

Graedon, Joe, and Theresa Graedon. *Graedon's Peoples' Pharmacy for Older Adults.* New York: Bantam, 1988.

Gunthrie, Donna. *Grandpa Doesn't Know It's Me.* New York: Human Sciences Press, 1986.

Heston, Leonard L., M.D., and June A. White. *Dementia: A Practical Guide to Alzheimer's Disease and Related Illness.* New York: Freeman, 1984.

Holland, Gail B. *For Sasha with Love: An Alzheimer's Crusade.* New York: Dembner Books, 1985.

Mace, Nancy L., and Peter V. Rabins. *The 36-Hour Day: A Family Guide to Caring for Persons with Alzheimer's Disease, Related Dementing Illnesses, and Memory Loss in Later Life.* Baltimore, MD: Johns Hopkins University Press, 1983.

Panella, John. *Day Care for Dementia.* White Plains, NY: Burke Rehabilitation Center, 1983.

Powell, Lenore S., and Katie Courtice. *Alzheimer's Disease: A Guide for Families.* Reading, MA: Addison-Wesley, 1983.

Reisberg, Barry, M.D. *A Guide to Alzheimer's Disease: For Families, Spouses and Friends.* New York: Free Press, 1983.

Roach, Marion. *Another Name for Madness.* Boston: Houghton Mifflin, 1985.

Safford, Florence. *Caring for the Mentally Impaired Elderly: A Family Guide.* New York: Holt, Rinehart and Winston, 1987.

Scully, Thomas, M.D., and Cynthia Scully. *Playing God: The New World of Medical Choices.* New York: Simon & Schuster, 1988.

Sheridan, Carmel. *Failure-Free Activities For the Alzheimer's Patient: A Guidebook for Caregivers.* Lake Bluff, IL: Quality Books, 1988.

U.S. Congress, Office of Technology. *Losing a Million Minds.* Washington, D.C.: Government Printing Office, 1987.

Zarit, Steven H., Nancy K. Orr, and Judy M. Zarit. *The Hidden Victims of Alzheimer's Disease: Families Under Stress.* New York: New York University Press, 1985.

GLOSSARY

acetylcholine a chemical that acts as a neurotransmitter in the brain and peripheral nervous system; the blockage of the action of acetylcholine can impair the ability to retain new and recall old information, a symptom characteristic of Alzheimer's disease

acetylcholine agonist any chemical that mimics the activity of the neurotransmitter acetylcholine

adrenal glands a pair of complex organs located near the kidney that produce sex hormones and hormones concerned with metabolic functions

amyloid an abnormal protein found in the brains of Alzheimer's patients and heavily concentrated in the core of neuritic plaques

angiopathy any abnormal condition of the blood vessels; people with Alzheimer's disease often suffer congophilic angiopathy, which is the deposition of amyloid material in the walls of the blood vessels

anticholinesterase a chemical that inhibits the activity of the enzyme acetylcholine; because a primary defect in Alzheimer's disease is the lack of acetylcholine in specific regions of the brain, one route to treatment is to block the activity of acetylcholinesterase

antidepressant a type of medication used to combat depression; antidepressants do not directly restore the cognitive functions of Alzheimer's patients, but they may partially improve the patient's thought processes by reducing the apathetic state associated with depression

autoimmune hypothesis the theory that Alzheimer's disease is caused by an abnormal immune reaction to some natural substance in the brain; most Alzheimer's experts do not believe there is sufficient evidence to support this idea

cerebral cortex the area of the brain that governs higher functions, such as thought and language

choline acetyltransferase (CAT) an enzyme essential to the production of the neurotransmitter acetylcholine; a greatly decreased amount of CAT in the cortex is a symptom of Alzheimer's disease

cholinergic hypothesis the theory that the primary brain defect in Alzheimer's disease is the loss of neurons that receive messages via the neurotransmitter acetylcholine

chromosome rodlike structure found in the nucleus of mammalian cells that contains the genes; each human cell (except gametes) contains 23 pairs of chromosomes

cognitive functions mental activities—such as memory, thought, and judgment—that are considered to be higher functions of the human brain

computerized axial tomography (CAT scan) a procedure for producing a cross-sectional, computer-generated, composite X-ray picture of the body or of an organ; it is sometimes useful for distinguishing Alzheimer's disease from other conditions that can cause dementia

contracture a permanent shortening of muscle tissue that produces a distortion or disfiguration

dementia mental deterioration resulting from an organic or functional disorder

Down's syndrome congenital mental and physical disorder caused by a chromosomal anomaly; the incidence of Down's syndrome is increased among families of people who have early-onset Alzheimer's disease

ergoloid mesylates a mixture of plant-derived chemicals related to natural bodily hormones; one formulation of ergoloid mesylates is FDA approved for treatment of dementia

familial Alzheimer's disease (FAD) a form of Alzheimer's disease with an early onset (many victims are in their forties), a rapid course, and a strong genetic link; children of FAD patients have a 50% chance of getting this form of the disease

Hydergine an ergoloid mesylate thought to improve the metabolism in brain cells by increasing the blood supply to the brain; directly stimulating the metabolism may improve alertness and elevate energy and mood

immune system the body's mechanism for combating viruses, bacteria, and other outside threats; composed of two types of white blood cells (phagocytes, which consume bacteria, and lymphocytes, which produce antibodies)

kuru a rare disease found among primitive tribes in New Guinea; its destruction of brain cells leads to mental deterioration

lecithin a natural substance that can be converted in the body to choline, a form of vitamin B, and used by the body to manufacture acetylcholine

lesion an abnormal change in an organ or tissue caused by illness or injury

magnetic resonance imaging (MRI) a diagnostic procedure in which pictures of the organs and tissues inside the body are obtained through the use of powerful magnetic fields instead of X rays

mentally incompetent a court-determined state in which a person is judged no longer capable of handling his or her own legal and financial affairs

multi-infarct dementia a condition in which multiple small strokes or hemorrhages scattered throughout the brain destroy mental capacities

neuritic plaques abnormalities in the brains of Alzheimer's patients visible under a microscope; plaques are composed of clusters of degenerating nerve endings located mainly in the cerebral cortex, the part of the brain used in memory processing

neurofibrillary tangles brain abnormalities characteristic of Alzheimer's disease; tangles contain materials that are also found in fibers or filaments present inside healthy nerve cells

neuroleptic a type of medication used to treat psychotic patients, primarily schizophrenics; neuroleptics are sometimes useful in treating agitation or violence in Alzheimer's patients

neuron the fundamental functional unit of neural tissue found in both the brain and in the nerves of the limbs, trunk, and spinal cord of the body; a neuron consists of a central body from which extend synaptic connections to other nerve cells or to muscles

neuropathologist one who studies abnormalities of the brain and the nervous system

neurotransmitter a chemical that is released by neurons and transmits nerve impulses across synapses

night wandering a type of behavior, typical of people in the advanced stages of Alzheimer's disease, in which the patient has difficulty sleeping and wanders about at night

Parkinson's disease a disorder of the nervous system in which muscle movement slows and tremors occur; the disease, usually found in the elderly, is caused by a deficiency of the chemical dopamine, which acts as a neurotransmitter

positron emission tomography (PET) a form of imaging that uses very low doses of radioactivity to measure metabolic activity in the brain
pernicious anemia a blood disorder caused by impaired ability to absorb vitamin B_{12}
power of attorney a legal arrangement in which a person designates a friend, relative, or other trusted person to handle financial or legal matters
pseudodementias illnesses in which cognitive functions are impaired but not primarily due to brain damage; they may result from depression, kidney disease, too much medication, or a toxic combination of medications

respite care a form of care in which an Alzheimer's patient is periodically cared for by someone other than the primary care giver, usually trained persons from a social service agency

senility the state in which an elderly person loses his or her cognitive faculties
somatostatin a chemical "messenger" greatly decreased in the cerebral cortex of persons with Alzheimer's disease, causing inability of brain cells to communicate

tranquilizer a form of medication that relieves anxiety

vasopressin a natural hormone in the body that may have some ability to enhance memory

INDEX

PICTURE CREDITS

AP/Wide World Photos: pp. 17, 18, 19, 21, 39, 42, 43, 44, 47, 54, 76, 84, 87; The Archives of the Mount Sinai Medical Center: p. 68; Food & Drug Administration: p. 63; Bob Gomel: pp. 13, 27, 72, 83; Edward Hauser/NYT Pictures: p. 71; Merrell Dow Pharmaceuticals, Inc.: p. 64; National Institute on Aging: pp. 34, 39; National Institutes of Health: pp. 29, 32, 51, 57, 59, 60; National Library of Medicine: p. 23; M. M. Rotker/Taurus Photos: pp. 40, 41; U.S. Bureau of the Census: p. 20; Visiting Nurse Service of New York: p. 81; Original illustrations by Gary Tong: p. 35

William A. Check, author of *AIDS* in the Chelsea House ENCYCLOPEDIA OF HEALTH and *Drugs of the Future* and *Drugs & Perception* in the Chelsea House ENCYCLOPEDIA OF PSYCHOACTIVE DRUGS, holds a Ph.D. in microbiology from Case Western Reserve University. He is coauthor of *The Truth About AIDS*, which won the American Medical Writers' Association Book Award, and a frequent contributor to medical reports for the National Institutes of Health and the Office of Technological Assessment.

Dale C. Garell, M.D., is medical director of California Childrens Services, Department of Health Services, County of Los Angeles. He is also clinical professor in the Department of Pediatrics and Family Medicine at the University of Southern California School of Medicine and Visiting associate clinical professor of maternal and child health at the University of Hawaii School of Public Health. From 1963 to 1974, he was medical director of the Division of Adolescent Medicine at Children's Hospital in Los Angeles. Dr. Garell has served as president of the Society for Adolescent Medicine, chairman of the youth committee of the American Academy of Pediatrics, and as a forum member of the White House Conference on Children (1970) and White House Conference on Youth (1971). He has also been a member of the editorial board of the *American Journal of Diseases of Children.*

C. Everett Koop, M.D., Sc.D., is Surgeon General, Deputy Assistant Secretary for Health, and Director of the Office of International Health of the U.S. Public Health Service. A pediatric surgeon with an international reputation, he was previously surgeon-in-chief of Children's Hospital of Philadelphia and professor of pediatric surgery and pediatrics at the University of Pennsylvania. Dr. Koop is the author of more than 175 articles and books on the practice of medicine. He has served as surgery editor of the *Journal of Clinical Pediatrics* and editor-in-chief of the *Journal of Pediatric Surgery.* Dr. Koop has received nine honorary degrees and numerous other awards, including the Denis Brown Gold Medal of the British Association of Paediatric Surgeons, the William E. Ladd Gold Medal of the American Academy of Pediatrics, and the Copernicus Medal of the Surgical Society of Poland. He is a Chevalier of the French Legion of Honor and a member of the Royal College of Surgeons, London.